MORE PRAISE FOR *The Meditator's Atlas*

"Flickstein's valuable instructions on the posture, place, and time
dedicated to sitting meditation will motivate both the beginning
and experienced meditator to a more dedicated practice."
—*Hsi Lai Journal of Humanistic Buddhism*

"Flickstein's commentary on *The Path of Purification,* one of the most
penetrating yet practical teachings of the Buddha, brings an imme-
diacy and insight that are valuable aids to its study."
—*The Beacon*

"A brilliant resource."
—Jim Lassen-Willems, Vipassana teacher

"Flickstein has managed to select what is essential and clarify
this dense and complex material, but without watering it down.
The heart of it is all there. I know how valuable this will
be to serious practitioners of dhamma."
—Barbara Brodsky, Deep Spring Center for
Meditation and Spiritual Inquiry

"Remarkably clear and straightforward, *The Meditator's Atlas*
provides an authentic and pragmatic framework for
understanding this amazing journey of awakening."
—Joseph Goldstein, author of *One Dharma*

ALSO BY MATTHEW FLICKSTEIN: *Journey to the Center*

"There are very few books that can change the lives of
their readers. Journey to the Center is one of them."
—Stanley Krippner, Professor of Psychology, Saybrook Institute

"Destined to become a classic in the Insight meditation tradition."
—*Shambhala Sun*

"The kind of book that can change a person's life and point the way to greater peace and happiness."
—Bhante Gunaratana, author of *Mindfulness in Plain English*

"A must for those who wish to understand the union between psychology and spirituality from inside their own lives."
—Ginny Morgan, Director, Mid-America Dharma Group

"Matthew writes with intelligence, simplicity, and respect. Wherever you are on your journey, you will find yourself in these pages, supported, challenged to grow, and even entertained."
—Sarah Sadler, Director, Evergreen Cove Holistic Learning Center

"Provides a significant and meaningful approach to living in and reaching beyond our day-to-day existence."
—Rabbi Martin Siegel, Chaplain for Amtrak

"The workbook format makes the meditations easy to follow, simple to do, and very effective. Flickstein leads readers to uncover unconscious memories, discover new, positive ideas, and open the way to change. *Journey to the Center* is a guide to successful living."
—*New Age Retailer*

"A book to do rather than simply to read, to be worked with slowly and intensely but also joyfully."
—*NAPRA ReView*

"Matthew Flickstein gave me the catalyst I needed; his approach is fresh, gentle, and comforting."
—Linda Loewenthal, One Spirit Book Club founding editor

THE MEDITATOR'S ATLAS

THE MEDITATOR'S ATLAS

A Roadmap of the Inner World

Matthew Flickstein

Foreword by Bhante G.

Previously published as *Swallowing the River Ganges*

Wisdom Publications • Boston

Wisdom Publications
199 Elm Street
Somerville MA 02144 USA
www.wisdompubs.org

Library of Congress Cataloging-in-Publication Data
Flickstein, Matthew.
  The meditator's atlas : a roadmap of the inner world / Matthew Flickstein ; fore-
word by Bhante G.
      p. cm.
  Based on Buddhaghosa's Visuddhimagga.
  Revision of Swallowing the river Ganges.
  Includes bibliographical references and index.
  ISBN 0-86171-337-0 (pbk. : alk. paper)
  1. Religious life—Buddhism. 2. Meditation—Buddhism. I. Buddhaghosa. Visud-
dhimagga. II. Flickstein, Matthew. Swallowing the river Ganges. III. Title.

BQ5395.F55 2007
294.3'4435—dc22

                                                        2006039692

ISBN 0-86171-337-0

11 10 09 08 07
5   4   3   2   1

Cover design by Tony Lulek with thanks to Jim Zaccaria. Interior design by Tony
Lulek

Previously published as *Swallowing the River Ganges.*
Wisdom Publications' books are printed on acid-free paper and meet the
guidelines for permanence and durability of the Production Guidelines for
Book Longevity of the Council on Library Resources.

Printed in the United States of America

♻ This book was produced with environmental mindfulness. We have elected to
   print this title on 50% PCW recycled paper. As a result, we have saved the following resources: 14 trees, 10 million BTUs of energy, 1,217 lbs. of greenhouse
gases, 5,053 gallons of water, and 649 lbs. of solid waste. For more information,
please visit our website, www.wisdompubs.org

To Bhante Gunaratana —

A meditation master who illuminates

the path of purification

through his words, thoughts, deeds, and silence

CONTENTS

FOREWORD

In this book, *The Meditator's Atlas*, Matthew Flickstein takes you on a guided tour of the "Path of Purification" as laid out in the great classic of Buddhist literature called the *Visuddhimagga*.

The Buddha's teachings rest on three pillars: morality, concentration, and wisdom. The seven stages of purification, as discussed in the *Visuddhimagga (Path of Purification)*, reinforce and strengthen these three pillars from the beginning of our practice to the point of perfect enlightenment. Morality, concentration, and wisdom are inextricably linked together, and their interdependency is systematically presented throughout all of the Buddha's discourses.

The teachings in the *Visuddhimagga* begin with purification of virtue since the completion of the path to liberation rests squarely on the foundation stone of morality. This point cannot be over-emphasized.

The importance of the purification of virtue is illustrated in the first two stanzas of the *Dhammapada*:

> All actions are led by the mind;
> mind is their master, mind is their maker.
> Act or speak with a defiled state of mind,
> And suffering will follow
> As the cart-wheel follows the foot of the ox.

All actions are led by the mind;
mind is their master, mind is their maker.
Act or speak with a pure state of mind,
And happiness will follow
As your shadow follows you without departing.

In other words, if our actions and speech are rooted in greed, hatred, or delusion, our mind feels burdensome, like an ox struggling to pull a cart filled with merchandise. The ox feels no pleasure in his work but has no choice since he is yoked to the cart and forced to work by the driver. In the same way, a lack of virtue tends to makes our lives more complicated and keeps us in bondage to psychological and spiritual pain.

On the other hand, if our actions are rooted in generosity, loving-kindness, and wisdom, our mind feels light and free—unfettered, just like our shadow. If we cultivate virtue, then comfort, peace, and joy are our constant companions—just as our shadow never departs from us.

Purification does not come from outside of ourselves. No one can purify another. The *Dhammapada* says, "By oneself committing evil does one defile oneself; by oneself not committing evil does one become pure. Purity and impurity depend on oneself. No one can purify another."

Although morality is the foundation of the entire path, we cannot stop there. In order to experience true peace and happiness, we must also develop the subsequent stages of purification. This is expressed as the threefold excellence of the teaching of the Buddha: excellence at the beginning (morality); excellence in the middle (concentration); and excellence in the end (wisdom).

The path of purification is the basis of a happy life. Following the path of purification, however, is not a "quick fix."

It takes much effort, but the result is worth it. As we purify ourselves, we experience greater and greater happiness as a result
of our practice. One of the main teachings of the Buddha is
that one gains faith in the practice by directly experiencing the
results of one's own efforts.

Quite often, we are asked to explain or describe the final
goal of spiritual practice; this is not easy to do. When we follow
any type of path, we gradually move closer to our final destination. Taking only the first step is not enough; nor can we
skip or rearrange steps. Even when we are very close to the
goal, we are still unable to truly describe it. We must walk all
the way from the beginning to the end to truly understand
what is at the end of our journey.

Similarly, we cannot become complacent when we experience one of the seven stages of purification. There is still more
work to be done. By following the entire path, we can slowly
eliminate the qualities of mind that hinder the attainment of
freedom. Every step of the path is necessary to arrive at our
destination—spiritual liberation.

Matthew Flickstein's presentation of the path of purification is
more concise and accessible than the more technical explanation found in the *Visuddhimagga*, the standard commentary on
the Buddha's teachings. The examples Matthew uses to illustrate his points are modern ones. This is a fresh, contemporary
presentation of a venerable and ancient teaching. Matthew's
understanding of his topic is traditional, but vital and practical. The *Visuddhimagga* is the work of an ancient Buddhist
scholar, written for scholarly monastic students of meditation.
Matthew's presentation here is for the current-day student,
who may be unfamiliar with the Pali language and the technical subtleties of ancient scholars. As evident in his talks and

previous writings, Matthew is a very effective communicator. He is a man who can convey his deep knowledge of the Buddha's Dhamma in a more comprehensive and concise way than many other contemporary writers.

Matthew's training as a psychotherapist and a seasoned meditation teacher has beautifully equipped him to deal lucidly with a subject that is often written about in obscure, scholarly jargon. I am sure the readers of this book will find that it profoundly deepens their practice.

Bhante Henepola Gunaratana
Bhavana Society Monastic Center

PREFACE

I have always enjoyed reading maps. They hold the promise of lands not yet explored and of adventures not yet experienced. Some maps represent the physical world and others represent the world of ideas. *The Meditator's Atlas: A Road Map of the Inner World* clearly describes the Buddha's path of purification, one of the most profound and practical maps of the spiritual dimension of life.

This path precisely reveals the beliefs, ideologies and thought processes that act as roadblocks along our journey to achieving spiritual liberation. But more importantly, it fully describes the specific insights which act as guideposts, affirming to each student that he or she is indeed on the direct path to the attainment of liberation.

In the spiritual domain, our thought processes can act as filters or perceptual distortions that preclude us from realizing the deepest spiritual realities. When we cease believing that our mental overlays reflect the ultimate reality of life, we begin to experience the freedom that lies at the end of our journey. This is not freedom "from" something, but the freedom that comes from living without the self-constructed boundaries that limit our experience of peace, joy, and love.

The Meditator's Atlas will enable those who are dedicated to following the path to spiritual realization to apprehend that no separation exists between themselves and the very truths they are seeking. The ultimate goal of this book is to enable you, the reader, to follow this road map of the inner world to the first-hand experience of spiritual freedom.

ACKNOWLEDGMENTS

The depth of my gratitude toward my wife, Carol, knows no bounds. She patiently edited numerous versions of the manuscript and offered invaluable insights and suggestions concerning its content. Her consistent encouragement and support have been a blessing to me and have transformed my life.

Friendships and wise counsel are key to progressing on the spiritual path. Walter Schwidetzky and Ginny Morgan have offered both throughout the creation of this book. The writings and talks of Bhikkhu Bodhi have greatly influenced my thinking about the *Path of Purification*. I am deeply grateful for his contribution in this regard, and for his significant contribution to the spread of Dhamma throughout the world.

THE PATH OF PURIFICATION

THE UNFOLDING OF AWARENESS

One of the most transformational insights that arises as a result of practicing the principles outlined in the *Path of Purification* is the realization of the inherent lawfulness of the purification process. When the causes and conditions that lead to spiritual purification are intentionally cultivated, spiritual liberation naturally follows. The teachings in the *Path of Purification* act as a map that describes with great precision the specific mental factors leading to spiritual purification. They also provide a comprehensive description of the purifications to which these mental factors lead.

As a child, I lived near a penny arcade. I spent much of my time, and pennies, playing a "safe driver" game. The objective was to keep a small car in the middle of a winding road by maneuvering the steering wheel, which was attached to the car by means of a long metal rod. The road was painted on a rotating drum, and the longer the car remained on the road, the faster the drum moved. If the car swerved off the road, the drum stopped turning and you had to begin again.

The unfolding of awareness proceeds in a similar manner. As long as we remain on the path of purification, the momentum of

our practice increases and our understanding deepens. If, however, we deviate from the path, we produce results that arrest our
momentum and become impediments to the goal we are trying
to achieve.

In the Buddhist tradition, the ultimate spiritual goal is the
realization of *nibbana*—a transcendent reality that exists beyond
the laws of cause and effect. Although nibbana cannot be realized without having completed the purification process, nibbana does not arise as a result of the process. Nibbana is a
self-subsistent reality that is not the result of anything. By following the path of purification, we merely eradicate the delusions and perceptual distortions that prevent us from discerning
this ultimate truth.

THE SEVEN STAGES OF PURIFICATION

In the *Majjhima Nikaya*, the middle-length discourses of the
Buddha, there is a narrative entitled the "The Relay Chariots."
In this discourse, Sariputta, one of the Buddha's chief disciples, and the venerable Punna Mantaniputta are discussing the
path that leads to the realization of nibbana. During their
conversation, the following stages of purification are mentioned: purification of virtue; purification of mind; purification of view; purification by overcoming doubt; purification by
knowledge and vision of what is the path and what is not the
path; purification by knowledge and vision of the way; and
purification by knowledge and vision.

These stages of purification, however, are not elaborated
upon anywhere in the Buddha's discourses. The main source
for uncovering their precise meaning is the *Visuddhimagga* (literally, the "Path of Purification"). The *Visuddhimagga* is a detailed
commentary on the teachings of the Buddha. It was written by

Buddhaghosa, a fifth-century monk who lived in Sri Lanka.

The stages of purification are briefly described in the *Abhidhammatta Sangaha*, the main primer for understanding the *Abhidhamma*—the systematic analysis of ultimate realities. This analysis thoroughly describes the relative and conditional realities of mind and matter, as well as nibbana, the absolute and unconditioned actuality. However, the discussion of the stages of purification in the *Abhidhammatta Sangaha* is merely a review of what is described in the *Visuddhimagga* and contains no further explanation.

The purity to be attained at each stage of purification is manifested when we eradicate the unwholesome mental factors that oppose its arising. Purification of virtue is obtained by abstaining from unskillful speech and conduct, adhering to the principles of right livelihood, using our material goods wisely, and guarding our sense doors. Purification of mind is secured by ridding our mind of the hindrances to concentration. Purification of view is gained by eliminating wrong views, especially the view that there is a permanent self at the core of our being. Purification by overcoming doubt is obtained by realizing the conditioned nature of the entire phenomenal world, including our "subjective" experience of it. Purification by knowledge and vision of what is the path and what is not the path is generated by overcoming our attachment to the alluring experiences that arise in the course of practicing insight meditation. Purification by knowledge and vision of the way is achieved by aligning the mind with the factors of enlightenment that lead to our realization of nibbana. Purification by knowledge and vision is obtained when the mental defilements are eradicated as the supramundane paths are attained.

The Buddha taught specific practices that support the arising of each of the stages of purification. Many of these practices are described in one of the most important discourses given by the Buddha, the *Mahasatipatthana Sutta*, or the "Great Discourse on the Foundations of Mindfulness." In this discourse, the Buddha describes precise techniques for a thorough examination of our psychophysical organism from four distinct perspectives: from the perspective of the body, from feelings, from states of consciousness, and from *dhammas* (generally translated as "mental objects").

Table 1 lists the seven stages of purification and some of the essential practices that when cultivated enable us to realize each of the purifications. The correlation of the stages of purification with the practices discussed in the *Mahasatipatthana Sutta* is not described in the *Visuddhimagga* or in the *Mahasatipatthana Sutta* itself. This precise application of individual practices to the stages of purification developed out of my experience in working with meditation students over the years.

The realization of each stage of purification naturally leads to the unfolding of the next. During the purification process we experience a sequence of sixteen insights, which counter sixteen erroneous views. These insights start to arise at the stage of purification of view, when we begin the practice of insight meditation. With the attainment of nibbana, our minds are in direct relation to the seventh and last purification, purification by knowledge and vision. The key insight associated with this final stage of purification is referred to as the knowledge of the supramundane paths.

The experience associated with each stage of purification is self-validating. One does not need a teacher to know which insights have been achieved; however, a teacher can provide a frame of reference for the student's experience. Further, because of the unusual and sometimes frightening nature of insights experienced, a teacher can offer guidance, support, and encouragement when necessary.

TABLE 1
STAGES OF PURIFICATION AND RELATED PRACTICES

Stage of Purification	Related Practices
1. Purification of virtue	Ethical principles of living
2. Purification of mind	Development of concentration
3. Purification of view	Initial insight training
4. Purification by overcoming doubt	Mindfulness of the body and feelings
5. Purification by knowledge and vision of what is the path and what is not the path	Mindfulness of consciousness and dhammas
6. Purification by knowledge and vision of the way	Choiceless awareness
7. Purification by knowledge and vision	Focus on impermanence, unsatisfactoriness, or selflessness as a doorway to the unconditioned

THE FRAMEWORK PROVIDED BY THE FOUR NOBLE TRUTHS

The Four Noble Truths present a coherent description of reality from both the relative and absolute perspectives. These truths act as a blueprint that reveals states of mind that perpetuate a life fraught with dissatisfaction, as well as states of mind that lead to psychological and spiritual freedom. In addition to containing all the teachings of the Buddha, the Four Noble Truths provide the framework for the path of purification.

How many times have you tried to change self-destructive or self-defeating behavior patterns, only to find that you were unable to make those changes, or to sustain the changes once they were made? Perhaps you wanted to modify your eating habits, to maintain an exercise plan, to stop smoking, or to become less emotionally reactive to petty irritations. Although cognitively aware of the need to abandon old habits, the forces that prevented you from making those changes may have been stronger than your will to implement them.

The ability to manifest immediate and permanent behavior modifications, however, often comes about after we encounter significant trauma in our lives. For example, individuals who survive heart attacks may immediately stop smoking, change their diet, begin to exercise, and learn stress management techniques to deal with their emotional difficulties. The capacity to make meaningful changes when a trauma is experienced reflects a psychological principle: It is only when the pain of perpetuating old behavior patterns is perceived to be greater than the pain brought about by trying to change those patterns that we are able to effect and sustain significant psychological and behavioral modifications.

The Buddha understood this principle. Consequently, the First Noble Truth provides the motivation for change by setting forth a detailed exposition of the myriad ways in which life, as most people live it, is fraught with unhappiness and dissatisfaction. With the true realization of the range and depth of suffering experienced in our day-to-day lives, our will to implement change becomes strong enough for us to begin our journey toward spiritual liberation.

In the First Truth the Buddha illustrates how birth, aging, death, sorrow, lamentation, despair, physical pain, mental pain, meeting with unwanted people and circumstances, having to separate from people and circumstances that are desirable, and not getting what we want, are forms of suffering that we all experience from time to time. The Buddha also points to the

striking fact that the psychophysical organism, which we identify with as being our "self," is actually the ultimate source of
dissatisfaction in our lives. We cannot gain a sense of stability
or security in an uncertain world by clinging to a self that does
not actually exist.

When we begin to understand and acknowledge the scope
of suffering that we experience, we naturally question how we
can allay our psychic pain. The Second Noble Truth offers the
answer. It is not the circumstances of our lives in and of themselves that create our suffering, but the craving to have our lives
meet the demands of our self-serving egos. This craving manifests itself as the desire for sensual pleasures, the desire for
continued existence, and the desire for non-existence of
unpleasant experiences or of life itself when the travails of life
become overwhelming. Craving, along with every other aspect
of our lives, arises from certain causes and conditions. The Second Noble Truth describes in great detail the circumstances
that contribute to the arising of the three types of craving.

The Third Noble Truth flows naturally from the Second. It
reveals that by eliminating the craving from the deepest strata
of our minds, we will experience liberation from all forms of suffering and dissatisfaction. Liberation, or the psychological and
spiritual freedom referred to as nibbana, is not a negative state
in which there is merely the absence of suffering. It is a profound experience of peace and well-being that transcends the
boundaries of any and all mental constructs used to describe it.

In the presentation of the Third Noble Truth, the Buddha
is once again using a psychological principle to motivate the
listener to action. By presenting a glimpse of what it would be
like to have a mind free from the worry and stress that arise
from the vicissitudes of life, one is inspired to expend the effort
to attain equanimity and peace.

Nibbana itself is not the result of anything, since it is an unconditioned reality. The Fourth Noble Truth sets out specific behavioral and mental exercises, which when diligently followed lead to the elimination of the defilements that prevent us from experiencing this ultimate form of freedom.

The practices defined by the Fourth Noble Truth, referred to as the Noble Eightfold Path, are generally presented in three categories or groupings: morality, concentration, and wisdom. Although all three categories must be cultivated simultaneously, morality provides a strong base for the arising of concentration, and concentration is a necessary condition for the arising of wisdom. The morality category consists of right speech, right action, and right livelihood; the concentration grouping includes right effort, right mindfulness, and right concentration; and the wisdom section consists of right view and right intention.

If we overlay the stages of the path of purification onto the three divisions of the Fourth Noble Truth, we discover how the Four Noble Truths provide a framework for the path of purification. We see that purification of virtue corresponds to the cultivation of morality, purification of mind parallels the development of concentration, and the last five purifications coincide with the unfolding of wisdom.

PURIFICATION OF VIRTUE

To reach the pinnacle of spiritual realization, we must align every aspect of our lives with that goal. To do so, our spiritual practice must go beyond the time we devote to formal meditation. When the true scope of practice is not recognized, we risk engaging in behaviors that produce results inconsistent with our spiritual goals and sabotage the possibility of realizing the deeper stages of spiritual purification.

Many meditators, however, hold a limited view of practice, simply equating it with "time spent on the cushion." For example, several retreat centers have experienced problems with visitors stealing meditation cushions. Ironically, the cushions were taken to be used in the pursuit of enlightenment. Such behavior reflects confusion regarding the domain and range of spiritual practice.

When there is no separation between our practice and our day-to-day lives, our spiritual progress is accelerated. We can more readily penetrate the delusions that obstruct our capacity to recognize the true nature of experience. These delusions are perceptual distortions that reside in the mind and express themselves through our words, thoughts, and deeds.

Purification of virtue refers to the examination and, where appropriate, modification of our physical actions and interpersonal communication, in order to prevent the manifestation of mental defilements through their grosser forms of expression. This process entails rigorously observing the moral precepts prescribed by the Buddha, engaging in right forms of livelihood, cultivating a wise attitude toward the use of our material goods, and keeping vigilant guard at the sense doors.

If we went no further in our spiritual development than to purify our virtue, we would still experience many benefits. In the *Mahaparinibbana Sutta* ("The Discourse on the Great Passing"), the Buddha addresses householders and describes some of the advantages of leading a virtuous life: attainment of wealth due to careful attention to one's affairs; development of a good reputation; confidence to approach people; clarity of mind at the time of one's death; and the experience of a favorable rebirth. The ultimate benefit is the cultivation of a mind that is unstained by thoughts of remorse or regret and, therefore, supports the development of concentration and wisdom.

OBSERVING THE PRECEPTS

There are five basic precepts, or principles of living, that the Buddha prescribed for everyone. These precepts are a guide to behaviors that are either to be avoided, because they lead to unfortunate consequences, or to be cultivated, because they support spiritual development. By following these precepts, our actions and speech are aligned with those of enlightened beings. This alignment helps to foster states of mind that lead to the realization of ultimate truth. As you will discover, the precepts reflect a depth of spiritual practice that may not be initially apparent.

The first precept:
Avoid killing and act with reverence toward all forms of life.

This precept applies to the taking of our own life as well as to taking the lives of others. It means honoring and embracing all life forms, including those of insects and other creatures we may consider threatening, bothersome, or insignificant.

On a more subtle level, we need to recognize that we express a lack of reverence toward others when we communicate using harsh words, or by displaying offensive gestures and facial expressions. Whenever we make judgments about people—labeling them selfish, ignorant, arrogant, and so forth—we relate to those people as if they were fixed objects and "kill off" our connection to their individuality and inherently divine nature.

The second precept:
Avoid stealing and cultivate generosity.

The precept not to steal requires close examination of all our behaviors, so that we can adhere to this principle even in what appear to be trivial circumstances. Consider, for example, how you would respond to the following situations: If change were mistakenly returned after making a call at a pay phone, would you redeposit it? If you needed a paper clip or another common office supply, would you take it from a coworker's desk without first asking for permission? If you found money lying in the street and were unsure whether the owner would return searching for it, would you leave the money where you found it? The decisions we make when confronted with these types of circumstances have a significant bearing on the development of our character and the purification of our virtue.

The counterpoint to stealing is generosity. Most people, if asked, would say that they consider themselves generous. In reality, however, most of us have a difficult time "letting go." The generosity we do express may often be limited to the members of our immediate family.

When we forgo an opportunity to express generosity, it is generally because we are attached to our possessions or resources. Since we believe ourselves to be generous, we tend to justify our selfish actions. We may say that we do not have enough even for ourselves, that we may need in the future what we are thinking of giving away, that the recipient would not appreciate the value of our gift, and so forth. To cultivate a generous heart we must begin by recognizing the depth of our attachments and by realizing what makes us resistant to opening our hearts in this way.

The following exercise will help to uncover any personal barriers to expressing generosity: Make a determination to give away one of your most cherished possessions. It could be a painting or sculpture that you created, a valuable coin that you purchased, or a book that cannot easily be replaced. It is important to be sure that you will no longer have access to the object once it is given away.

After you make the decision about what to give away and whom to give it to, watch for signs of resistance. Listen for subtle justifications for not completing the exercise. Finally, carefully observe any grief that may arise as a consequence of no longer having the possession to which you were attached.

The experience of resistance, justification, and grief are the mind states that need to be countered in order to increase our capacity to express generosity. The starting point is to become mindfully aware of these mental states whenever they arise.

For some individuals, giving of their time is more difficult than giving away material goods. To spend time with someone who is ill, in pain, or who frequently complains can be very trying. However, this form of generosity is closely associated with compassion and is extremely worthwhile to cultivate.

The third precept:
Avoid sexual misconduct and be considerate
in intimate relationships.

Sexual misconduct includes rape, adultery, and other obviously inappropriate sexual encounters. On a more subtle level, we need to avoid any activities in which we relate to others as objects of sexual desire—such as watching pornography, talking about our physical attraction to others, and making sexual innuendoes through our words or actions.

Consideration in regard to our intimate relationships pertains to less obvious forms of sexual misbehavior. For example, if one person in a relationship is not inclined toward sexual intimacy, his or her partner needs to respect those wishes and act accordingly. Attempts to persuade one's partner to be intimate or to use sexual intimacy as a bargaining chip in the relationship demonstrates a lack of consideration and is regarded as a breach of this precept.

The fourth precept:
Avoid lying and relate what is true while remaining
sensitive to the potential impact of all communication.

Following this precept is of key importance to our spiritual development. To fully keep this precept, we need to recognize the impact our words have on others. We need to avoid expressing what we consider to be "harmless" lies, to make sure that what we say is consistent with what we do, and to immediately communicate changes in circumstances that prevent us from keeping commitments we have previously made. Our lives must be in alignment with truth at every level for spiritual understanding to arise.

We also need to investigate how truthful we are when we listen to others. We compromise our integrity when we give the outward appearance of listening, but are actually thinking about something else. Although the individual speaking to us may not be consciously aware of what is occurring, by virtue of this subtle communication disparity, the speaker has an intuitive sense of not having really been heard. We need to train ourselves to remain as present and open as possible while listening to what others are saying.

The Buddha speaks of four categories of communication and our responsibility regarding each category: saying something that is untrue and displeasing to hear (such as false accusations) should never be done; voicing something that is untrue but pleasing to hear (such as flattery) should also be withheld; saying something that is true but displeasing to hear (such as constructive criticism) should only be spoken when the person is receptive to what is being said; and finally, communicating something that is true and pleasing to hear (such as positive feedback) should also be withheld until the timing is suitable. The Buddha's words point out that for communication to have integrity and to be effective, we need to consider both the content and timing of that communication.

The fifth precept:
Avoid intoxicants, which confuse the mind and cause
heedless behavior, and ingest only those substances
that are nourishing and supportive of peaceful abiding.

We need to abstain from using alcohol and drugs, which weaken our mental faculties and ultimately lead to unskillful actions. On a more subtle level, we need to avoid exposing our minds to less obvious intoxicants—such as movies, books, and television programs that are filled with images of sexuality, violence, and the search for sensual gratification. Allowing these images to run unimpeded through our minds affects our thinking process and can lead to unwholesome behaviors.

During retreats, or at other times specifically devoted to spiritual development, it is helpful to take the following, more rigorous, set of precepts. These eight precepts support the arising of the wholesome mental states that lead to concentration and wisdom:

1. Avoid killing and act with reverence toward all forms of life.

2. Avoid stealing and cultivate generosity.

3. Avoid engaging in activities that focus on sensual experience, and keep the mind directed toward spiritual development.

4. Avoid speaking and keep noble silence.

5. Avoid intoxicants, which confuse the mind and cause heedless behavior, and ingest only those substances that are nourishing and supportive of peaceful abiding.

6. Avoid overeating and eat only at appropriate times.

7. Avoid activities that arouse the emotions and scatter the mind, and work on developing concentration.

8. Avoid slackening our resolve, and focus on attaining liberation.

The initial two precepts, avoiding killing and stealing, are the same as the first two basic precepts we discussed previously. Precepts three through five are modifications of the basic precepts to avoid sexual misconduct, lying, and the use of intoxicants. The final three precepts address behaviors that are especially relevant to a retreat environment.

When on retreat, there is ample opportunity to practice each of the precepts. For example, we can practice the first precept, acting with reverence toward all forms of life, when our meditation is disturbed by annoying insects, barking dogs, or by other retreatants who cough or shift positions, making noises that interfere with our concentration.

As a consequence of having limited exposure to sense stimuli during a retreat, food becomes a major source of craving and attachment. We can practice generosity, the second precept, by allowing others to step ahead of us in the food line, or by taking the smaller of two portions offered.

The third precept, not engaging in sexual misconduct, is expanded to encompass the commitment to avoid activities that focus on sensual experience. This includes refraining from hugging or touching others, since such behaviors tend to arouse sense desire. Retreatants also agree not to apply perfumes, colognes, or makeup, which are primarily used to enhance our appearance or personal appeal.

The fourth precept, not lying, is broadened and becomes the training precept of not speaking and of maintaining "noble silence." Retreatants are also encouraged to avoid eye contact. Limiting verbal communication and other forms of social interaction enables us to focus more of our efforts on spiritual development.

During retreats, the fifth precept, avoiding intoxicants, can be expanded to include caffeine in addition to alcohol and drugs. Stimulants tend to create physical and emotional spikes that interfere with our endeavor to achieve tranquillity.

While meditating, there are times when the mind experiences extreme boredom. As a result, we tend to create fantasies that act as mental intoxicants. Dwelling on these fabricated visions should be avoided since they are impediments to concentration and to the arising of insight.

Abiding by the sixth training precept, not engaging in the type of eating that impedes meditation, helps to avoid sleepiness, fatigue, and a drowsy mind, all of which act as hindrances to the development of concentration. For example, since the digestive process drains energy that can otherwise be used in the service of meditation, we should modify our diets by eating foods that are more nourishing and easier to digest. We can also take smaller servings since we require less food when we sit in meditation for extended periods of time. If we continue to take our usual portions, we find ourselves fighting sleep during meditation sessions. Finally, we can skip the evening meal, or take only light refreshments at that time. This enables us to meditate more comfortably during the evening hours.

The training precept of not engaging in activities that arouse the emotions or scatter the mind addresses the temptation to act on sense desires. It is difficult to observe the breath (or any other object of meditation) for extended periods of time without the mind beginning to crave sensory stimulation and emotional excitement. The desire to listen to music, read, study, plan, write, or to enjoy the natural beauty surrounding the retreat center arises soon after the retreat begins. To maintain this precept, it is helpful to reflect on the priceless opportunity we have to deepen our practice. Appreciating that such an opportunity may not arise again during our lifetime can strengthen our determination to use every moment of the retreat experience for the advancement of our spiritual understanding.

The final training precept, not slackening our resolve, involves maintaining clear intention and commitment. The clarity and strength of our intentions are directly related to the quality of our behaviors, and ultimately, therefore, to the results we achieve. This does not mean, of course, that we should avoid napping or feel guilty every time we lose our focus during a retreat. Making a commitment to practice diligently at the beginning of a retreat helps to keep us motivated and acts as a compass that keeps us traveling in the right direction.

ENGAGING IN RIGHT FORMS OF LIVELIHOOD

For many of us, a major part of our identity is tied up with the type of work that we do. Our careers provide a means of self-expression, an opportunity to feel connected to the rest of the world, a vehicle for making a contribution to society, and a way to support our families. When we meet someone for the first time, the conversation almost inevitably turns to "What do you do for a living?" Many of us spend more time at work than with our friends and families. Because of the emphasis that we place on our work, it is not surprising that the Buddha focused on this aspect of our lives when he discussed the purification of virtue.

When the Buddha described right livelihood as part of the Noble Eightfold Path, he advised us to earn our living by honest means. He cautioned us to avoid doing harm to others either during the performance of our work, or as a result of the work that we perform. If upon reflection, we discover that there are elements of deceit or harm in the work that we are doing, we need to eliminate such unwholesome practices. If this is not possible, we are advised to choose another career.

The Buddha discussed five specific forms of livelihood to be avoided that directly or indirectly bring harm to others: dealing in weapons; dealing in living beings, which includes slavery, prostitution, and raising animals for slaughter; dealing in meat production or butchering; dealing in poisons; and dealing in the production or sale of intoxicants.

Doing harm to others through our livelihood often takes place on more subtle levels. There are individuals who earn their living by taking people fishing or hunting. While they may not fish or hunt themselves, they are supporting the killing of living beings.

There are business organizations where competitors are considered the enemy, and strategies are devised to eliminate them. Although no physical harm is implied, this kind of attitude cultivates hatred and division, which can ultimately lead to unskillful speech and actions.

At times, our work may involve less obvious forms of deception. For example, a surgeon who had been reflecting on right livelihood related that he was searching for a new specialty. He felt that he could no longer, in good conscience, play the role of a physician who knew all the answers; he could no longer assure his patients that the surgeries he suggested would alleviate their problems.

A podiatrist communicated that she worked for a doctor who encouraged her to decrease the amount of time she spent with each patient so that her caseload would increase. She was also requested to suggest more elective surgery, which would generate additional revenue for the practice.

There are sales organizations that make exaggerated claims about their products or services. Some salespeople attempt to close sales by playing on the fears and vulnerabilities of prospective clients.

Employers may be deceiving their employees by not providing them with adequate pay or by not offering them promotions that they have earned. Employees may be deceiving their employers by engaging in personal projects while on company time, by not performing their duties conscientiously, or by taking home supplies that belong to the organization.

To support the cultivation of virtue, we need to reflect on our behaviors and attitudes with regard to our own careers. If you were to discuss your career with the Buddha himself, what aspects would you be hesitant to mention, perhaps because you question the ethics of your actions or the purity of your intentions? We need to deeply consider this question to be sure that we are truly engaged in right forms of livelihood.

CULTIVATING A WISE ATTITUDE TOWARD MATERIAL GOODS

Material goods are the things we use to support our lives and to protect ourselves from undesirable environmental influences. They include the food we eat, the clothes we wear, the homes we live in, and the medications we ingest. When the Buddha taught that we should cultivate a wise attitude toward material goods, he was indicating that we should use them skillfully.

The use of material goods gives rise to sensory experiences, which we may find pleasurable. There is nothing inherently wrong with the enjoyment of sensory experiences. Our world is filled with pleasant sights, sounds, smells, tastes, touches, feelings, and ideas. Sensory experiences only become impediments to our spiritual growth when we grasp at them, believing that they belong to us or that they are an intrinsic part of our being.

Of all material goods, food is the one that appears to be at the forefront of most people's minds. We spend much of our lives considering, discussing, preparing, and eating food. Food can become a major issue for people, resulting in eating disorders, overeating, obesity, or obsessive preoccupation with dieting.

Food provides us with a great deal of sensual satisfaction. We consider food one of life's simple pleasures and see nothing wrong with being moderately obsessed with its consumption or enjoyment. Any obsession, however, is an impediment to the development of concentration, which is the next stage of spiritual purification.

The Buddha suggested that we consider food comparable to medicine, which is used to keep our bodies healthy, enabling us to continue with our spiritual development. In a sutta called "The Greater Discourse at Assapura," the Buddha advises how we should reflect on our food prior to eating our meals:

> We will be moderate in eating. Reflecting wisely, we will take food neither for amusement nor intoxication nor for the sake of physical beauty and attractiveness, but only for the endurance and continuance of this body, for ending discomfort, and for assisting the holy life, considering: "Thus shall I terminate old feelings (of hunger) without arousing new feelings (of having overeaten) and I shall be healthy and blameless and shall live in comfort."

We need to closely examine the way in which we use material goods in order to determine if we are using them skillfully. Rather than abandoning the use of any material goods, we need to develop a wholesome attitude toward their use. We can, for example, consider whether we are wearing particular items of clothing to call attention to our bodies, whether we are decorating our homes to impress others, whether we are wearing specific items of jewelry to demonstrate our wealth, or whether we are using our automobiles to make a statement about our sexuality.

At first glance, the intentional consideration of whether we are using our material goods wisely may not seem directly related to the purification of virtue or to the development of spiritual understanding. However, using material goods to derive sensual pleasure or to project a certain image in the world keeps our minds focused outwardly. The development of concentration and wisdom requires an inward focus, and cultivating a skillful attitude toward material goods begins to point us in the right direction.

GUARDING THE SENSE DOORS

According to Western psychology, there are five sense organs, which experience corresponding sense objects. The eye sees forms, the ear hears sounds, the nose smells odors, the tongue tastes flavors, and the body feels tangible objects. Buddhist psychology considers the mind to be the sixth sense organ, which experiences mental objects such as thoughts and emotions, and acts of volition. The six sense organs are referred to as "doors," since they are the portals through which all sensory experiences arise to consciousness.

Consciousness is the bare awareness of sense objects as they present themselves through the six sense doors. Although it appears that we remain conscious all of the time, in reality, what we are experiencing are moments of consciousness, which are appearing and disappearing at infinitesimally small intervals. A film appears to be seamless when it is projected onto a movie screen, but is actually comprised of individual frames. The speed with which the frames are projected onto the screen creates the illusion of a continuous flow. Similarly, the speed with which consciousness rises and falls creates the appearance that it is present as an ongoing experience.

Each moment of consciousness can only have one sensory experience as its object. In other words, we cannot be aware of more than one sense object at a time. Although it may appear, for example, that we are seeing and hearing simultaneously, there is actually a rapid alternation of moments of consciousness with either a sight or sound as the object of each of those moments.

A specific sequence of events transpires whenever we have a sensory experience. The first part of this sequence is automatic and occurs without any conscious consideration on our part. Whenever a sense organ comes into contact with a sense object, and consciousness is present, that experience results in the arising of a feeling. A feeling in this context is not an emotion, but rather the experience of that sense object as pleasant, unpleasant, or neutral. For example, when we become aware of a bird singing, the awareness will most likely result in the experience of a pleasant feeling; when we twist our ankle, it will most likely cause an unpleasant feeling; and when we look at a building that we pass every day on our way to work, it will most likely produce a neutral feeling.

As a result of feelings that arise, an untrained mind—one that does not recognize the presence of sensory experiences or the feelings that correspond to those experiences—will react in one of three ways: it will grasp after a pleasant object or the feelings that are derived from that object; it will resist the experience of an unpleasant object or the feelings that result from that object; or it will become dull, lethargic, or bored with a neutral object or the feelings that stem from that object. This reactivity perpetuates the delusion that exists in our mind.

It is possible, however, to become consciously aware of our sensory experiences and the feelings that arise as a consequence of those experiences. By doing so, we can short-circuit the mind's automatic and conditioned reactivity. The process of intentionally introducing this type of awareness is referred to as "guarding the sense doors."

Of all forms of activity that help to purify our virtue, guarding the sense doors is the one most commended by the Buddha. Following the precepts, maintaining a right form of livelihood, and developing a wholesome attitude toward the use of material objects all help us cultivate virtue in a global sense. However, guarding the sense doors is a practice that works to purify our virtue on a moment-to-moment basis.

What determines whether a thought, word, or deed is unwholesome (unskillful) or wholesome (skillful) is the intention behind the action being performed. If activities are motivated by forms of greed, hatred, or delusion, they are considered unskillful. If, on the other hand, they are motivated by forms of generosity, loving-kindness, or clarity of mind, they are considered skillful. Guarding the sense doors enables us to eliminate the reactive and unskillful responses to our sensory experiences and to introduce a response in keeping with skillful intentions.

The type of awareness that guards the sense doors and prevents a conditioned reactivity to the feelings that arise from our sensory experiences is called mindfulness. Mindfulness is a nonjudgmental awareness of what is happening to us and within us during successive moments of experience. Mindfulness acts as a wedge of awareness that allows us to examine and recognize the true nature of each experience as it arises to consciousness, without reacting to those experiences based upon our prior conditioning. As a result of mindfulness, we are able to respond to our experiences in skillful ways.

When we discuss the third stage of purification, purification of view, we will describe mindfulness in greater detail and explore various ways to cultivate it. When we review the fifth stage of purification, purification by knowledge and vision of what is the path and what is not the path, we will examine a second method of guarding the sense doors.

We have been emphasizing how important the purification of virtue is to our spiritual development. However, some meditators can develop concentration and experience insights even though their virtue is not fully purified. If we were to climb a mountain with a heavy pack on our back, we would still be able to make some progress on our journey. At the higher altitudes, however, where the air is thin and it is difficult to carry even our own weight, we would have to leave the heavy pack behind and take only what was essential in order to complete the climb. Similarly, we are able to make some spiritual progress even though we have not completed the first stage of purification. However, to realize the more profound levels of spiritual development, we must leave behind the burden of a mind that is weighed down by unskillful speech and actions, along with the unfortunate results those words and deeds tend to bring in their wake.

PURIFICATION OF MIND

The purification of virtue, as with all intentional actions, functions as both a cause and an effect. As a cause, it is responsible for changing our attitudes and behaviors. We begin to follow specific ethical guidelines and to cultivate a quality of mind that enables us to skillfully respond to our moment-to-moment sensory experiences.

As an effect, the purification of virtue manifests as states of mind unstained by thoughts or feelings of remorse. As a result of committing unwholesome actions or of not committing wholesome ones, a mind not purified through virtue frequently experiences a nagging sense of guilt. A mind thus filled with regret cannot fully concentrate, which is a necessary prerequisite for the purification of mind.

The importance of concentration to the development of wisdom cannot be overemphasized. Although various teachers have differing points of view on just how much concentration is needed to enable a meditator to cultivate insight, there is clear agreement as to the overall importance of concentration to moving further along the spiritual path.

LEVELS OF CONCENTRATION

Everyone has the ability to concentrate to some degree; the mental factor of attention is present during every moment of experience. However, the capacity to maintain concentration once it arises varies with each individual. Some people find it difficult to sustain concentration for even short periods of time, while others can flow from task to task without losing their focus. However, the degree of concentration that we experience in our day-to-day lives is not sufficient for the purpose of purifying our minds. The deeper levels of concentration needed are cultivated through the practice of meditation. We will be discussing how to practice both serenity meditation (*samatha*) and insight meditation (*vipassana*), each of which has different but complementary objectives.

When we practice serenity meditation, our minds become deeply concentrated and we experience profound feelings of calm. The two levels of concentration associated with serenity meditation are access concentration and absorption concentration. The state of consciousness that arises when absorption concentration is reached is referred to as a *jhana*. Some meditators consider the ability to dwell in these wholesome states of mind the only goal of meditation, while for others these exalted states of consciousness are seen as stepping stones leading to the practice of insight meditation.

Insight meditation enables us to penetrate our perceptual distortions and to see the true nature of experience. It leads to the end of suffering and to the direct realization of psychological and spiritual freedom. The level of concentration that is required for this type of meditation is called momentary concentration.

What makes these forms of concentration capable of purifying the mind is their capacity to suppress specific mental

factors, which, if not suppressed, act as hindrances to the arising of calm and insight. These five factors are sense desire, ill
will, sloth and torpor, restlessness and remorse, and doubt.
Since sloth and torpor are closely related, as are restlessness
and remorse, they are each counted as one factor. When we
reach access, absorption, or momentary concentration, the
hindrances are suppressed; however, until we have reached
these levels of concentration, we need to learn how to deal
with the hindrances in skillful ways. We will examine specific
techniques for working with the hindrances when we discuss
purification of view, the next stage of purification.

PRACTICING MINDFULNESS OF BREATHING
FOR CONCENTRATION

The Buddha described forty objects of meditation that can be
used to develop concentration. Most insight meditation teachers have their students begin by focusing on the breath as their
initial object of awareness. A principal reason for this choice is
that mindfulness of breathing can be used for cultivating
insight, as well as for developing concentration. The instructions for meditation that we will be following are from a discourse given by the Buddha: the *Mahasatipatthana Sutta*, or "The
Great Discourse on the Foundations of Mindfulness," to which
we briefly referred in the first chapter.

Before he delineated the specific instructions for meditation, the Buddha discussed the circumstances most conducive
to achieving success in the practice. He advised:

Having gone to the forest, to the foot of a tree, to a
secluded place, (one) sits down cross-legged, keeps his

upper body erect, and directs his mindfulness to the object of his meditation.

In this passage, the Buddha referred to three key elements: the ideal places in which to meditate, the posture to be assumed, and the intention that we are to keep in mind. The place we choose for meditation needs to be quiet, secluded, and as far from sensory distractions as possible. If we are unable to go to the forest, a meditation center, or a comparable environment, we should find a quiet place in our homes where we will not be disturbed. It is best to choose a time to meditate when no one else is up and around.

To assume the ideal posture, we are to sit either on the floor using a hard cushion placed on top of a mat, on a meditation bench, or on a straight-back chair. If we choose to sit on the floor, we can utilize any one of the four traditional meditation postures: the full-lotus (figure 1), the half-lotus (figure 2), the quarter-lotus (figure 3), or the uncrossed position (figure 4). For all of the floor positions, it is helpful to sit on the first third of the cushion (figure 5). This makes it easier for our knees to touch the mat, which creates a more stable posture. If we

Figure 1: Full-lotus

Figure 2: Half-lotus

Figure 3: Quarter-lotus

choose to sit on a straight-back chair (figure 6), we can insert a cushion between our back and the rear of the chair. Our feet should be placed firmly on the ground.

In all cases, our posture is straight but relaxed. It is important to keep our spine erect to prevent physical discomfort, sleepiness, and having our posture interfere with the natural flow of our breath. One hand is palm up and placed in our lap with the other hand, also palm up, on top of the first. Our eyes are usually closed, although some meditators prefer to keep their eyes open and cast downward with an unfocused gaze. We attempt to remain as still as possible during the entire meditation period, since movement tends to interfere with our concentration.

Our intention during meditation is to maintain an awareness of our meditation object at all times. A strong intention intensifies our efforts and helps us to focus our energies on the task at hand. Cultivating the mental quality of intention is key to achieving the optimal results from our meditation practice.

Decide on how long the meditation session will be before beginning. If possible, meditate for a minimum of twenty minutes. We can gradually work our way up to an hour, or even

Figure 4: Uncrossed

Figure 5: Proper positioning
on the cushion

Figure 6: Proper positioning
on a chair

longer. It is essential that we begin each meditation period with a sense of joy and an appreciation for the opportunity to practice in this way. Joy is a mental factor that directly supports the arising of concentration.

At this point we are ready to review the Buddha's instructions, from the *Mahasatipatthana Sutta*, for practicing mindfulness of breathing.

Ever mindful he breathes in, ever mindful he breathes out.

Begin by closing your mouth and breathing through your nose. Become aware, or mindful, of the tactile sensation of each breath as it flows in and out of the nostrils. Do not follow the breath as it moves through the body or out into space. Avoid trying to control the breath in any way. Stay focused solely on the tactile sensation of each in- and out-breath.

In other words, when the mouth is closed and the breath passes through the nostrils, the passage of air creates a sensation that can be felt either inside the nostrils, at the rim of the nostrils, at the tip of the nose, or on the upper lip. The touch-point varies for each individual. To help locate the place where we experience the tactile sensation most distinctly, we inhale deeply and force the air out through our nose once or twice. Wherever we feel the tactile sensation most clearly and precisely is the place to focus our attention.

In between each in-breath and each out-breath, and in between each out-breath and each in-breath, there is a short interval of time when the tactile sensation will be absent. During these periods we are to keep our attention focused on the place where the tactile sensation is normally felt, waiting for the return of the breath.

We want to become aware of each in-breath and out-breath

as it occurs. However, it takes time to develop the capacity to concentrate. Counting the breaths can assist us in generating this continuous awareness. The counting is to be done in our minds, without vocalizing the numbers.

With the sensation of our first in-breath, count "one." As the sensation of the out-breath is experienced at the touch-point, count "two." With the next in-breath, count "three." Keep counting in this manner until five breaths are counted. However, only count those breaths for which the tactile sensation has at least partially been discerned. When the mind becomes distracted and we lose complete track of any breath, we simply exclude that breath from the counting sequence and continue the count with the next in-breath or out-breath.

Whenever the mind loses track of any breath, it is important to be gentle but firm about bringing the attention back to the breath once again. Try to avoid self-judgment concerning the difficulty of maintaining concentration on the breath. Training the mind takes time and patience. Take it one breath at a time.

Immediately after counting the fifth breath, regardless of whether it was an in-breath or an out-breath, begin a new sequence of counting. We start at number one, but this time we count until six breaths are experienced. Continue increasing the count by one breath during each round of counting until reaching a sequence of ten breaths. We then begin the next round, counting only until reaching the fifth breath, as we did at the beginning of the process.

The purpose of the counting technique is to stop the mind from wandering, and to begin training the mind to remain wherever it is placed. We continue with the counting method until we are able to perceive each breath in any one sequence (five breaths, six breaths, and so on), without having any of them completely escape our attention. If our concentration is sufficient, there is no need to use the counting method. Some meditators find that they are able to immediately begin their practice with the next phase of the meditation process.

> Breathing in a long breath, he knows, "I am breathing in long." Breathing out a long breath, he knows, "I am breathing out long." Breathing in a short breath, he knows, "I am breathing in short." Breathing out a short breath, he knows, "I am breathing out short."

We persevere with our efforts to deepen concentration by noticing or "knowing" the length of each in-breath and each out-breath. In this context, *knowing* does not mean "thinking." It is a nonverbal awareness of the sensation of breathing as each breath is experienced at the touch-point. Be careful not to manipulate the length of the breaths or try and make them more forceful in an attempt to observe the breaths more easily. Just allow each breath to breathe itself.

The length of our breaths tends to vary from moment to moment and from meditation session to meditation session. At the beginning of any practice period, the breath may feel short, quick, or shallow. As concentration improves and the body and mind become more tranquil, the breath may feel longer, slower, deeper, or subtler. Our very awareness of the breathing process has a tendency to calm the breath. The *Visuddhimagga* provides an analogy to illustrate how the breath becomes more and more subtle as we begin to know it. It compares the process to hearing the progressively softer sounds of a gong after it has been struck.

Experiencing a more refined quality to the breath is an indication that concentration has improved, and that the mind is calmer. This indication that a greater degree of concentration has been reached is technically referred to as an acquired sign. We acquire a sign of increased concentration as a direct result of our efforts.

> "Making clear the entire in-breath body, I shall breathe in," thus he makes efforts. "Making clear the entire out-breath body, I shall breath out," thus he makes efforts.

When we are able to maintain an awareness of the length of each breath for several minutes, it is time to move on to the next stage in our development of concentration. In this passage, the Buddha is making reference to the breath body, and not to the physical body. We are to become aware of the beginning, middle, and end of every in-breath and of every out-breath. As with knowing the length of each breath, "making clear" refers to the nonverbal awareness of the sensation of breathing as each breath is experienced at the touch-point.

Some commentators interpret this particular instruction to mean that we are to follow the breath as it moves into and out of the physical body, so that we become aware of the relationship between the physical body and the breath. This type of effort is not necessary. As we pay close and consistent attention to the in-breaths and out-breaths, maintaining our awareness exclusively at the touch-point, we will automatically become conscious of the entire cycle of breathing and of how the breath affects the physical body. It is, in a sense, similar to peripheral vision, which enables us to know what is going on outside of our direct field of vision.

The words "shall" and "effort" are used by the Buddha to indicate that additional exertion is required to perceive the entire breath body. When first attempting this exercise, meditators may only be able to experience the beginning of each breath before becoming lost in another object of attention. Some may only be able to experience the middle of each breath, and others only the end. We are to notice at what stage in the breathing process we tend to lose our ability to stay present with each of our breaths, and to increase our effort at that point until each breath is seen in its entirety.

"Calming the activity of the breath body, I shall breathe in," thus he makes efforts. "Calming the activity of the breath body, I shall breathe out," thus he makes efforts.

As we remain present with the entire extent of each in-breath and each out-breath, the breath becomes even more refined. Unlike other objects of meditation, which become clearer as we focus upon them, the breath becomes more subtle and increasingly difficult to detect as our mind calms down. We may even reach a point where we are not sure if we are still breathing. Although in this passage the translation appears to indicate that we should intentionally calm the breaths, this is not the case. As we have been pointing out, the breathing process calms down on its own as we continue to focus upon it.

If our breath does quiet to the point that it feels as if the breathing process has ceased, fear or anxiety may arise. It is helpful, if that occurs, to reflect on the fact that we are still conscious and are quite alive. The reason we cannot perceive the breaths is because our concentration is not strong enough. If we keep our focus on the touch-point and make a concerted effort, we will be able to perceive the breathing process once again.

As the more subtle breaths become clear, a new indication or sign of deepening concentration may arise. A mental image, such as a bright light, a clear or colored disk, a cluster of stars, a flower, a gem, or a string of pearls may appear in the mind. The manifestation of any of these images is referred to as a *counterpart sign*. It is the mental counterpart to the physical experience of the subtle breath. The counterpart sign is usually accompanied by pleasant sensations, which can be described as joy or delight.

The degree of concentration present when the counterpart sign appears is referred to as the "access level of concentration." It is the stage of concentration that occurs prior to attaining the jhanas. The jhanas are profound states of consciousness that arise when a still deeper level of concentration, called "absorption," is attained.

With the arising of access concentration, the mental factors that act as hindrances to both the development of calm and insight are simultaneously suppressed. At this stage in our practice, an important choice point is reached. We can either continue with serenity meditation, experience the jhanas, and use that attainment for the basis of developing insight, or immediately begin practicing insight meditation (see table 2, on the following page).

Insight meditation can begin during any stage in the development of concentration. We can even initiate this form of meditation immediately after subduing the wandering tendencies of the mind through the use of the counting technique. However, our progress in achieving insight is quite dependent upon our capacity to concentrate well. The stage at which access concentration is experienced becomes an effective transition point because we have finally reached the phase of concentration at which the hindrances are under control.

When we begin practicing insight meditation, we focus on the impermanent, conditioned, and selfless nature of our

TABLE 2

HOW THE BREATH CAN BE USED
FOR PRACTICING SERENITY AND INSIGHT MEDITATION

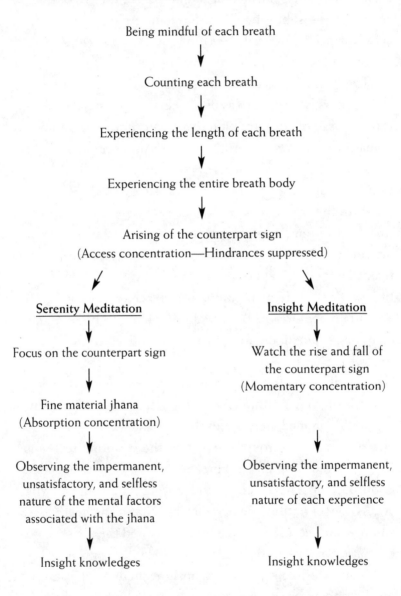

Being mindful of each breath

↓

Counting each breath

↓

Experiencing the length of each breath

↓

Experiencing the entire breath body

↓

Arising of the counterpart sign
(Access concentration—Hindrances suppressed)

Serenity Meditation

↓

Focus on the counterpart sign

↓

Fine material jhana
(Absorption concentration)

↓

Observing the impermanent,
unsatisfactory, and selfless
nature of the mental factors
associated with the jhana

↓

Insight knowledges

Insight Meditation

↓

Watch the rise and fall of
the counterpart sign
(Momentary concentration)

↓

Observing the impermanent,
unsatisfactory, and selfless
nature of each experience

↓

Insight knowledges

experience. Instead of excluding everything from our focus except for the main object of our attention, as we do with serenity meditation, we begin to utilize every object of consciousness as an opportunity to generate insight. Rather than sinking into the experience of a single object, such as the breath, we want to ride the crest of the waves of our experiences as they unfurl from moment to moment. When the access level of concentration is applied in this manner, it is referred to as momentary concentration, since it stays present with what is occurring in each new moment of experience. It is important to note that momentary concentration will ultimately arise on its own as we practice insight meditation, even if we begin practicing prior to achieving access concentration. We will describe the process of insight meditation more fully in our discussion of the purification of view.

When the counterpart sign initially arises, it is still very fragile. To continue with serenity meditation, we have to shift our attention from the breath and fix it directly on the sign. We need to apply great effort to make the sign clearer and to extend its range. It is essential that our living environment support the arising of absorption concentration and the mental factors that comprise the jhanas. We need to have nourishing food, a comfortable climate, a suitable place in which to meditate, and access to a teacher who can guide us.

In many of his discourses, the Buddha spoke of the virtue of fully achieving the jhanas prior to practicing insight meditation. He proclaimed their value in making the mind a more effective vehicle for the cultivation of insight. However, unless we have an extended period of time to devote to the practice of serenity meditation, and have the proper environmental and teaching support, we face an extremely difficult challenge when we pursue the attainment of these jhanas.

There are four different classifications of jhanas: the fine material jhanas, the immaterial jhanas, the vipassana jhanas, and the supramundane jhanas. The four fine material jhanas, referred to simply by numbers one through four, arise by virtue of using the counterpart sign as their basis. They are designated as fine material jhanas since the counterpart sign is a very refined and subtle sensory experience.

The four immaterial jhanas are designated as the base of boundless space, the base of boundless consciousness, the base of nothingness, and the base of neither perception nor non-perception. They are called immaterial because they transcend all perceptions of material form. They are specifically named after the immaterial basis of their attainment. A discussion of these jhanas is beyond the scope of this book.

The vipassana jhanas are states of consciousness that are associated with momentary concentration. They provide the mind with the ability to move from object to object, while observing the universal characteristics of impermanence, unsatisfactoriness, and selflessness. The vipassana jhanas use matter, consciousness, mental formations (the three conditioned realities), and nibbana (the unconditioned reality) as their objects of attention. When the vipassana jhanas have nibbana as their object, they are referred to as the supramundane jhanas. In the following chapters, we will focus on the vipassana jhanas and the insight knowledges that arise in dependence upon the attainment of these jhanas.

THE MENTAL FACTORS
ASSOCIATED WITH THE FIRST JHANA

As we continue to focus on the counterpart sign, with the hindrances remaining suppressed, certain mental factors that were present during the access stage of concentration in a less evolved form begin to rise into prominence. These five mental factors—applied thought, sustained thought, rapture, happiness, and one-pointedness of mind—are the qualities of mind that constitute the first jhana.

Applied thought is the capacity of the mind to strike at an object. The object at which it strikes in the context of attaining the first jhana is the counterpart sign. It strikes at the counterpart sign with enough power that the mind, with the aid of the mental factor of sustained thought, has the ability to become absorbed in that object. As each jhanic factor arises, it directly counters a specific hindrance. Applied thought opposes the hindrance of sloth and torpor.

Sustained thought is the factor responsible for the mind's ability to keep attending to an object once applied thought places it there. Sustained thought investigates, examines, and experiences the object of its attention. The *Visuddhimagga* provides similes that illustrate the difference between applied and sustained thought. Applied thought is like striking a bell; sustained thought is like the ringing that follows.

Applied thought is similar to the hand holding a tarnished dish; sustained thought is similar to the process of rubbing it clean with the other hand. The quality of sustained thought inhibits the hindrance of doubt.

Rapture, sometimes translated as "ecstatic joy," is experienced as a strong energy in the body. It arises as the mind takes a pleasurable interest in the meditation object due to the presence of applied and sustained thought. Although it has the effect of tranquilizing or calming the body, rapture has the defining quality of excitement in contrast to a feeling of peace. There are five different grades or depths of rapture: minor, momentary, showering, uplifting, and pervading. Minor rapture may be experienced as goose bumps or the rising of the hair on the body. Momentary rapture is a more dramatic thrill, but it does not last very long. Showering rapture feels like waves of energy repeatedly running through the body, like waves of water rushing to the shore. Uplifting rapture is so exhilarating that it can reportedly cause the body to levitate. Pervading rapture, the form of rapture associated with the jhanic state, fills the entire body with a sense of bliss as water fills a sponge to the point where it can contain no more. Rapture acts to suppress the hindrance of ill will.

Happiness is a pleasant feeling of great peace and calm. Since it does not have the excitement or stimulation associated with rapture, it is ultimately a more gratifying experience. Rapture and happiness are closely connected but there are qualitative differences. The commentaries offer an analogy that illustrates the difference: Suppose a traveler is walking across the desert and runs out of water. He sees an oasis, and great delight comes to his mind. He runs to the water, and after immersing himself in it, he takes a drink. He sits down to rest and feels great peace and ease. The excitement and delight that arose when seeing the oasis is similar to the arising of rapture. The great peace and ease he felt after enjoying the water is like the experience of happiness. The quality of happiness counters the hindrance of restlessness and remorse.

The final jhanic factor is one-pointedness of mind. This essential factor works to eliminate all distractions that prevent the mind from focusing on its object. It is present in all states of mind, but in the context of reaching a jhanic state, it is directed toward the counterpart sign, which is considered a wholesome object of attention. One-pointedness of mind subdues the hindrance of sense desire.

The jhanic factors arise one at a time and in the order indicated. As each factor arises, it becomes a support for the factor that succeeds it. However, for the jhanic state to arise, all five factors must be present simultaneously.

When all five jhanic factors have arisen with the simultaneous suppression of the hindrances, we have achieved the first jhana, or state of absorption. The next step is to develop mastery over the jhana. This involves cultivating five abilities relative to the jhana: entering into the jhana at will, remaining in the jhanic state as long as desired, emerging from the jhana at will, clearly isolating each jhanic factor after emerging from the jhana, and investigating the jhanic factors that have been isolated. We have now reached another important choice. We can either continue with serenity meditation and cultivate the second jhana, or use the first jhana as the basis for developing insight.

If the choice is made to begin practicing insight meditation, we need to recognize that upon emerging from the jhanic state, the mental factors that comprised that state are no longer present. The next step is to examine each of the jhanic factors to discover that while they are sublime, they still reflect the three universal characteristics of experience: impermanence, unsatisfactoriness, and selflessness. In this way, we have reoriented our focus from practicing serenity meditation to once again practicing insight meditation.

We are now ready to begin the exploration of the third stage of purification, purification of view. We will discuss this stage and the remaining stages of purification from the perspective of not having attained the first jhana, but of having reached the access level of concentration.

PURIFICATION OF VIEW

After developing sufficient concentration to calm the mind and temporarily suppress the hindrances, we are ready to shift our focus to the cultivation of insight. The heart of insight practice is investigating and ultimately eradicating the deeply held belief that there is a permanent and substantial core at the root of our personality around which the attributes of our body and mind cluster. This assumption or idea of a tangible entity that lies at the base of our experience is typically referred to as "I," "me," or "myself," or in more abstract terms as the self or ego.

Upon deep investigation we come to realize that what actually exists is an impermanent and selfless process that rises and falls according to causes and conditions. This process consists of five interdependent factors that are continually in flux. These factors are known as the five aggregates of clinging, because we cling to them with desire and with the erroneous view that they comprise a substantial self. These five aggregates are matter or material form, feelings, perceptions, mental formations, and consciousness.

Purification of view arises as a direct result of practicing insight meditation. This practice enables us to clearly recognize the impermanent and selfless nature of the five aggregates.

PRINCIPLES OF INSIGHT MEDITATION

In the *Mahasatipatthana Sutta*, before giving specific instructions for developing insight, the Buddha offered a set of guiding principles regarding the practices that were to follow. These essential principles are the backbone of insight meditation and are responsible for its effectiveness in purifying the mind. The Buddha said:

> Here, bhikkhus,
> a bhikkhu lives contemplating
> the body in the body,
> ardently, clearly comprehending and mindful,
> removing covetousness and grief in the world.

By using the word "here," the Buddha is pointing to the fact that the information he is providing in this discourse is from his perspective as a fully enlightened being. In effect, he is saying: "Here, from my point of view, as one who has completed the inner journey, the following is what I have come to understand."

The term "bhikkhu" usually indicates that the Buddha is addressing a monk. In the context of this sutta, however, it applies to anyone whose life is dedicated to spiritual freedom.

For many on the path to purification, spiritual discipline is a part-time pursuit. To show that life and practice must become one, the Buddha advises his listeners that an aspirant to spiritual liberation must continuously "live" in contemplation. The term "contemplation" refers to mindfulness and insight meditation, as opposed to mere cognitive reflection.

Understanding what the Buddha meant by "the body in the body" is key to the successful practice of insight meditation. This phrase points to the importance of making certain that we isolate the specific object of our meditation from other objects that may arise to consciousness during that time. When contemplating the body in the body, we avoid focusing on any feelings or thoughts that may surface in relation to the body. We are solely interested in observing the body as it presents itself to our awareness.

A second meaning for contemplating "the body in the body" is that we should not cling to the body as "I," "me," or "mine." Just as a microbiologist would observe a specimen on a slide without considering it part of his or her identity, one should merely observe the body as a material phenomenon that rises and falls based upon specific causes and conditions.

The word "ardently" refers to the application of energy, which is an important aspect of the meditation process. In general, it is the effort to remain focused on the object of meditation. When we find that we are losing our concentration, we need to apply more effort or energy until we are able, once again, to firmly hold our attention on the object we are trying to observe.

Specifically, there are three classifications of energy: inceptive energy, sustained energy, and courageous energy. Inceptive energy is the effort to move the mind back to the object of meditation each time concentration wavers. Sustained energy is the effort to keep the mind focused on the meditation object for extended periods of time. Courageous energy refers to the determination to stay present with physical or mental states that may be painful or frightening, and to avoid becoming attached to physical or mental states that may be alluring or exceptionally pleasant.

When we observe the body, or any other object of meditation, one of three characteristics intrinsic to that object (indeed, to all sense objects) needs to be recognized. That is, we need to notice either the impermanent, unsatisfactory, or selfless nature of that experience. When we discern one of these three characteristics, we are "clearly comprehending" the object of meditation.

Everything in the world of experience is impermanent. Our possessions, relationships, physical bodies, thoughts, and even consciousness itself are in a constant state of change. Yet, we cling to these phenomena as if they will last forever. Clearly comprehending impermanence means that we directly perceive the incessant rise and fall of every one of our sensory experiences. This does not suggest that we should think about how impermanent things are, but that we observe the truth of impermanence firsthand. When the fact of impermanence becomes clear to the mind, it stops its perpetual grasping and remains present with each new experience as it arises.

There are many pleasant experiences in life. What makes sensory experiences unsatisfactory is that they are impermanent and unable, therefore, to provide us with enduring happiness. The mind that has not clearly comprehended the unsatisfactory nature of sensory experience will keep clutching at each new sense object in a futile attempt to discover a permanent source of satisfaction. This relentless and frustrating process results in recurring feelings of anxiety and loss.

As we pay close attention to our moment-to-moment experience, we discover that all phenomena are in a perpetual state of change. Everything is always becoming other than it was just a moment before. Therefore, in actuality, it is not that everything is impermanent, but that impermanence is the only "thing" that there is. That is to say, if everything is continually changing, then no "thing" actually exists for even a moment in time. There is no self or permanent abiding essence as the basis of any experience. Words are merely symbols that act as conceptual overlays, giving the illusion of permanence to objects and experiences that are in a constant state of flux. The clear comprehension of selflessness is witnessing how our moment-to-moment experiences arise and pass away without the presence or necessity of a permanent self.

We do not need to recognize all three characteristics when observing the objects of meditation as they arise to consciousness. Since these characteristics are interrelated and interdependent, when we recognize the impermanence of an object, we are also seeing its unsatisfactory and selfless nature.

Mindfulness is a form of attention that has the capacity to observe what is happening to us and within us during each moment of experience. It is referred to as "bare attention" since it observes whatever is occurring bare of judgment, decision, and commentary. In other words, mindfulness is the direct observation of the meditation object without any of the distortions that normally arise from our cognitive processes.

The consequence of making judgments is to perpetuate obsessive patterns of mind. When we judge our mental processes to be positive or fortunate, we tend to grasp at them. By doing so these obsessive patterns of mind are reinforced. If we judge the contents of mind to be negative or unfortunate, we tend to resist them. Although the patterns will be suppressed, they will persist on an unconscious basis. Every form of judgment of or emotional reactivity to our patterns of mind actually invests them with additional power to influence us.

To be "bare of decision" means that, during the time devoted to meditation, we avoid planning or determining any future courses of action. If waves of creative ideas cross our mind, we need to resist the temptation to dwell on them. If we identify with the planning or creative process, the mind is not observing what is taking place in the here and now.

Keeping our attention "bare of mental commentary" means that we examine whatever arises during meditation without engaging in an internal dialogue. The mind has an opinion on everything, and we typically listen to the mind's comments because we believe that the mind may have something profound to say. However, it never does. Thoughts emerging from our established way of thinking are only variations on the same conceptual theme.

An *insight*, on the other hand, is a profound nonconceptual realization of the way things really are in the here and now. We can think about an insight after it occurs, but we cannot think our way into an insight. Insights illuminate the impermanent, unsatisfactory, and selfless nature of our moment-to-moment experience. When we pay bare attention to what is occurring, insights naturally arise on their own.

In the phrase "removing covetousness and grief in the world," the world to which the Buddha is referring is the one defined by the five aggregates of clinging: the material form of the body, feelings, perceptions, mental formations, and consciousness. "Covetousness" refers to greed, craving, or attachment; "grief" indicates anger, resistance, or hatred. By applying mindfulness or bare attention to our meditation object, covetousness and grief are temporarily eliminated. They are permanently eliminated when we reach an advanced stage of realization.

In summary, the principles that underlie the effective practice

of insight meditation include the following: the ability to recognize each moment of our lives as an opportunity for practice,
the capacity to keep focused on the object of meditation without becoming identified with it, the application of suitable
forms of effort, the comprehension of the three true characteristics of experience, the capacity to pay bare attention, and
the observation of our world of experience without attachment
or resistance. These factors must all work in harmony for
insight meditation to succeed.

There are also specific mental factors that must remain in
balance to achieve the optimal results from the practice of insight
meditation. The first two factors are faith (or confidence) and
discrimination. If there is too much faith, we may become emotionally carried away by thoughts of devotion or we may develop
unreasonable expectations regarding our teachers. On the other
hand, if there is too much intellectual discrimination or discernment, it may turn into undue skepticism and prevent us from
confidently moving forward with our practice.

Concentration and effort are the other two factors that
need to be in balance. If there is an excess of concentration, the
mind may become too tranquil and find it difficult to extend
the effort required to generate insight. If there is too much
effort without a sufficient degree of concentration, the mind
may become agitated and unable to focus, which would prevent us from seeing things as they really are.

It is the practice of mindfulness that is responsible for bal-
ancing each pair of mental factors. With its nonjudgmental
stance, and nonconceptual basis, this practice is perfect for the
task at hand.

THE ASSURANCE OF ATTAINMENT

When someone of the Buddha's spiritual stature gives a guar-
antee of enlightenment, we need to seriously consider what is
being said. There were only three occasions during the
Buddha's forty-five-year ministry when he offered this type of
assurance. One such occasion was when he presented the
Mahasatipatthana Sutta, the discourse on the four foundations of
mindfulness.

The Buddha told his listeners that "whoever is practicing
these four foundations of mindfulness in this manner for seven
years, he can expect one of two results—highest knowledge
here and now, or, if there is still a remainder of clinging, the
state of nonreturner." (The state of nonreturner is the third of
four stages of enlightenment.) After declaring the need for
seven years of practice, the Buddha progressively shortened
the amount of time needed until he ultimately told his listeners that enlightenment could be reached in only seven days.

However, by using the phrase "in this manner" as part of
the assurance, the Buddha related a key condition for the
attainment of enlightenment within this brief period of time.
The condition is that we practice the exercises from each of
the four foundations of mindfulness as explained in this sutta.
The four foundations are the mindful observation of the body,
of feelings, of consciousness, and of dhammas, sometimes
translated as mental objects.

It is essential to work with all four foundations because
the practices associated with each foundation directly counter
and ultimately eliminate four corresponding perceptual distortions that prevent the attainment of enlightenment. The
belief that the body is attractive and desirable and that it is a
worthwhile pursuit to have as much sensual contact with

other physical forms as possible is directly opposed by the mindful observation of the body. The notion that sensory experience can provide us with a lasting source of happiness or satisfaction is dispelled by the mindful observation of feelings. The conviction that our experiences maintain some degree of permanence is challenged by the mindful observation of consciousness. The view that there is a substantial self that lies at the root of our experiences is contradicted by the mindful observation of dhammas. It is, therefore, essential to work with all four foundations of mindfulness in our pursuit of spiritual freedom.

PRACTICING MINDFULNESS OF BREATHING FOR INSIGHT

Our prior discussion of mindfulness of breathing ended with instructions for "calming the activity of the breath body." To practice insight meditation, we continue to stay present with the full extent of each in- and out-breath, while applying the critical principles just reviewed: we keep focused on the breath without identifying with it as "our" breath; we make the effort to remain mindful of what is occurring during each new moment of experience, and we recognize the impermanent nature of each breath.

The difference in the way in which the breath is observed for the development of concentration versus the cultivation of insight is quite subtle. Watching the breath as a way to cultivate concentration is similar to keeping our focus on the flow of snowflakes as they fall from the sky. Our sole interest is on the process of snowing. Watching the breath to achieve insight, however, is similar to observing the individual snowflakes that make up the snowfall. We notice the snowflakes while still maintaining an overall awareness of the process of snowing. In other words, we observe the individual moments of experience comprising each breath, while still remaining present with the process of breathing.

After practicing in this manner for a period of time, it is inevitable that insights will begin to arise. The Buddha describes some of these insights in the following passages from the section of the *Mahasatipatthana Sutta* concerned with mindfulness of breathing.

> Thus, he lives contemplating the body in the body internally, or...the body in the body externally, or... the body in the body internally and externally.

"Contemplating internally" means that we have realized the impermanent nature of our own breaths. At some point an insight about other people's breaths may enter our mind: "Just as each of my in-breaths and out-breaths are impermanent, every other person's in-breaths and out-breaths are also impermanent." This is not a thought that is intentionally cultivated during meditation, but the spontaneous arising of an insight regarding the breaths of other individuals. The arising of this insight regarding the breaths of other people is referred to as "contemplating externally."

At times while we are contemplating our own breath, an insight about the universality of the breathing process may enter our mind; then we may immediately return to the contemplation of our own impermanent breath. When this sequence occurs in quick succession, it is referred to as "contemplating internally and externally."

> He lives contemplating the origination factors of the breath body, or he lives contemplating the dissolution

factors of the breath body, or he lives contemplating
both the origination and dissolution factors of the
breath body.

The origination factors are the specific elements of the
breathing process that are responsible for the arising of each
breath. These factors are the physical body, the nasal aperture,
and consciousness. An insight will occur to the meditator that
the breath is dependently arisen and will not arise in the
absence of any of these three factors. As before, this is not a
thought that we cultivate during meditation but the spontaneous arising of an insight. The dissolution factors are the
breaking up or disappearance of any or all of the same factors
that support the arising of the breath.

Two additional insights may occur to the meditator at this
point. The first is that everything that has the nature of arising has the nature of disappearing. The second is that when
the factors responsible for the arising of some experience disappear, the experience that was based upon those factors also
disappears.

When the contemplation of the arising factors and the dissolution factors occur in quick succession, this is considered
"contemplating the arising and dissolution factors of the breath
body." This contemplation leads to a deep understanding of
the impermanent and conditioned nature of all experience.

Or his mindfulness is established with the understanding that "only the breath body exists."

This statement of the Buddha implies two things. The first
is that we are to focus exclusively on the breath body; that is
to say, to contemplate the body in the body. If another object

of awareness arises that distracts our attention from the breath, we are to watch it rise and fall. We then gently but firmly return to the observation of the breath. The second meaning is that it is not "our" breath that is being observed. There is no man, woman, person, or self behind the process of breathing. The breath is just breathing itself. It arises based upon the origination factors previously discussed. The awareness that "only the breath body exists" is the realization of selflessness.

And that mindfulness is established to the extent necessary for further knowledge and mindfulness.

Mindfulness of the breath body is established for only one reason. It is meant to lead us to states of increased awareness and to clear comprehension of the true characteristics of experience. Clear comprehension leads, in turn, to the various insight knowledges and, ultimately, to spiritual freedom.

And he lives independent and clings to nothing in the world.

Once again, the world that the Buddha is referring to is the world defined by the five aggregates of clinging. Upon seeing the impermanent and selfless nature of the breath body, we stop clinging to it with craving or wrong views. As our practice of insight meditation proceeds, we will ultimately discover that there is no experience that is worthy of being clung to. The Buddha marks the end of his teachings on mindfulness of the breath body with the following statement:

Thus too, O bhikkhus, a bhikkhu lives contemplating the body in the body.

WORKING WITH THE FIVE HINDRANCES

As we mentioned earlier, when momentary concentration is present, the five mental factors that prevent the arising of concentration and insight (the five hindrances) are suppressed. When our concentration begins to wane, the hindrances resurface. When this occurs, we need to immediately and skillfully work to remove them from our mind.

The five hindrances are sense desire, ill will, sloth and torpor, restlessness and remorse, and doubt. As with all sensory experiences, they arise and disappear due to specific causes and conditions. To prevent these hindrances from arising and to effectively work with them when they do, we must understand the causes and conditions responsible for their appearance and for their disappearance.

The Buddha described two ways of reflecting upon our moment-to-moment experiences, either viewing them with unwise consideration or with wise consideration. We employ unwise consideration when we observe our experiences through any one of the four perceptual filters just reviewed: the belief that the body is attractive and desirable, the conviction that our experiences maintain some degree of permanence, the opinion that there are circumstances that can provide a lasting sense of happiness or satisfaction, and the view that there is a substantial core or self that lies at the root of our experiences. The five hindrances arise as a result of these unwise considerations.

The way to temporarily eliminate the hindrances from our mind is to practice wise consideration. (The hindrances are not permanently eliminated until the last stage of purification is realized.) We are using wise consideration when we observe the sense world as it truly is. Mindfulness enables us to gain this clear perspective.

Since consciousness can only have one object at a time, when mindfulness is applied, the hindrances are immediately removed from our awareness. Through the lens provided by mindfulness, we are able to recognize the impermanent, unsatisfactory, and selfless nature of each hindrance. The result is that we transform a potential stumbling block into a stepping stone for achieving a greater clarity of mind.

We may find, however, that in some cases our mindfulness is not strong enough to eliminate a hindrance from our consciousness. For those occasions, the Buddha suggested specific strategies to overcome each of the hindrances.

Sense Desire

Sense desire refers to the craving of or longing for pleasant sense objects such as delightful sights, sounds, smells, tastes, touches, and ideas. Sense desire keeps the mind captivated at a superficial level of attention. The pleasant feelings that can be experienced through sense contact reinforce the mind's desire to encounter and grasp at future moments of enjoyment.

If sense desire manifests as lust or longing for contact with other physical forms, the Buddha suggests contemplating the various parts of the body, reflecting on the stages of the body's decomposition after death, and considering how the body is merely composed of material elements. Creating disgust and aversion for the body is not the point of these practices; they are designed to help the meditator develop a realistic perspective regarding physical forms.

To overcome other forms of sense desire, we can practice guarding the sense doors as previously discussed. We mindfully watch the rise and fall of pleasant feelings that manifest as a result of sense contacts. In this way, we prevent the mind from grasping after pleasant feelings or the objects responsible for the arising of those feelings. Other suggestions include moderation in eating, hearing talks on the value of abandoning sense desires, and spending time with a teacher who models sense restraint.

Ill will

Ill will includes all negative evaluations of an object and all aversion to individuals and circumstances. Ill will can manifest as anger, resentment, hatred, antagonism, irritation, fear, anxiety, tension, or boredom.

As with sense desire, guarding the sense doors can be helpful in dealing with ill will. By mindfully watching the rise and fall of unpleasant feelings that manifest as a result of sense contacts, we can prevent the mind from resisting unpleasant feelings or the objects that are responsible for the arising of those feelings.

Making a determined effort to forgive ourselves for our own past wrongdoings, and to forgive those who have treated us badly in the past is also effective in dealing with ill will. To remove feelings of hatred the Buddha frequently suggested practicing meditations that focus on cultivating loving-kindness. These meditations involve wishing health, happiness, peace, and success for ourselves, our teachers, our friends and family, our enemies, and for all living beings.

Reflecting on the fact that we reap the results of our actions, and on the danger, therefore, of beginning a chain of events rooted in hatred or aversion, is another skillful way of working with ill will. Finally, it is helpful to have a good friend who models forgiveness, loving-kindness, and compassion.

Sloth and Torpor

Sloth and torpor refer to very similar traits. Sloth manifests as a dull and cloudy quality of mind; torpor arises as feelings of drowsiness. Almost all meditators experience this hindrance at some point. When overcome by sloth and torpor our mind loses track of the meditation object and we may even fall asleep.

If the other hindrances are not recognized as soon as they arise, the mind can still identify them at a later point in their development. The difficulty with sloth and torpor is that if they are not seen as soon as they arise, the mind becomes progressively duller and drowsier until we fall asleep and are, therefore, unable to recognize the presence of the hindrance. The best defense against sloth and torpor is to become aware of its presence the very moment it begins to arise. At that point we need to elevate the amount of effort or energy that we are applying. One way to accomplish this is to temporarily increase the number of objects to which we attend. We can alternate between experiencing the tactile sensation of the breath, becoming aware of the sensations associated with the sitting posture, experiencing the sensations connected with the hands touching one another, and so on.

To help prevent sloth and torpor, we should avoid overeating. When we overeat the energy that could be applied to meditation is used for the process of digestion. When we are feeling sleepy, we can meditate in a standing position, or begin walking meditation. Other suggestions include imagining a bright light in our mind, washing our face with cold water, or vigorously rubbing our limbs. If all else fails, we can take a short nap with the intention to begin meditating immediately upon awakening.

Restlessness and Remorse

Restlessness and remorse are linked because they are both agitated states of mind. Restlessness is experienced as an unsettled state of mind unable to remain on the object of meditation. It arises when we dwell on something that causes us to feel stress, anxiety, or inner turmoil. Remorse is experienced as a feeling of guilt or worry concerning something we did in the past or something we believe we should have done but did not do.

If a horse were in a stall and became agitated, we could calm the horse by putting it in a corral where it has more space to move. Similarly, to calm the mind it can be helpful to give our thoughts more space to express themselves, still observing them with mindfulness. By watching our thoughts with choiceless awareness, that is, without trying to control them in any way, they often come quietly to rest. The key is to not get carried away and create an internal dialogue based on the thoughts being observed. Other suggestions are to review the Buddha's teachings, which tend to have a calming effect on the mind, and to associate with friends who are virtuous and peaceful.

Doubt

The hindrance of doubt is expressed through skeptical questioning. We may question whether there really was an enlightened being whom we refer to as the Buddha, whether the teachings we are receiving are absolutely true, whether the teachings have become distorted after 2,500 years, and even whether the practice of meditation itself is effective. We may also doubt whether others who followed the path actually reached enlightenment and whether we have the ability to follow the path in the same way.

One way to work with doubt is to ask questions of someone who has confidence in the Buddha and his teachings. There is no need for blind faith in Buddhism. However, doubt can only be permanently eradicated by personally practicing the Buddha's teachings and discovering the truth for ourselves. As the Buddha said many times, "Come and see for yourself."

THE KNOWLEDGE OF DELIMITATION
OF MIND AND MATTER

As we continue practicing insight meditation, we will eventually experience sixteen specific insights, which are referred to as insight knowledges (see table 3). These insight knowledges define which stage of purification the meditator has achieved. The knowledge of the delimitation of mind and matter is what demarcates the purification of view.

The knowledge of the delimitation of mind and matter is the realization that the breath has both a material and a mental aspect to it. At this point we are able to distinguish the physical process of breathing from the mental act of noticing each breath. Further, each breath and the act of noticing is seen to rise and fall in pairs: in-breath/noticing, out-breath/noticing, in-breath/noticing, and so forth. Prior to the purification of mind and the development of momentary concentration, the mind was too consumed with focusing on the meditation object to become aware of its own processes.

At this stage we also begin to realize that when breathing occurs, nothing exists aside from the material process of breathing and the mental process of noticing the breath. The breath is recognized as an impermanent and dependently arisen process that appears and disappears without any self as part of the process.

Each insight knowledge arises as a direct experience and does not occur through reasoning or by "searching" for an insight. When the appropriate causes and conditions arise, insights naturally follow. The knowledge of the delimitation of mind and matter has arisen as a consequence of purifying our virtue and mind, and by applying the principles of insight meditation to the observation of our breath.

TABLE 3

THE SIXTEEN INSIGHT KNOWLEDGES

1. The knowledge of the delimitation of mind and matter

2. The knowledge of conditionality

3. The knowledge of comprehension

4. The knowledge of arising and falling away

5. The knowledge of dissolution

6. The knowledge of the fearful

7. The knowledge of danger

8. The knowledge of disenchantment

9. The knowledge of desire for deliverance

10. The knowledge of re-observation

11. The knowledge of equanimity toward formations

12. The knowledge of conformity with truth

13. The knowledge of change of lineage

14. The knowledge of the path

15. The knowledge of fruition

16. The knowledge of reviewing

OVERCOMING DOUBT

Although we are beginning to recognize that there is no self as part of our experience, it is natural to continue to have doubts about how the five aggregates can function without a self directing the process. These doubts are resolved when we realize the knowledge of conditionality and have, therefore, reached the stage referred to as purification by overcoming doubt. This stage of purification arises when the specific causes and conditions responsible for the ongoing functioning of the five aggregates are understood.

To discern for ourselves how this "dependently originated" process occurs, we will continue with the practices outlined in the *Mahasatipatthana Sutta*.

MINDFULNESS OF THE BODY

In addition to mindfulness of breathing, the contemplations in this section of the discourse include those on the postures of the body, as well as on developing clear comprehension, realizing the repulsive nature of the body, recognizing the material elements, and visualizing the stages of the body's decomposition after death occurs. Some of the contemplations concerned with learning to view the body realistically may appear grim and actually do run against the grain of what most people choose to reflect upon. It is important to acknowledge that these contemplations may affect the way in which we relate to the physical form of others, especially from a sexual perspective. The Buddha taught these contemplations for those who were intent on achieving liberation, no matter what the cost to their sensual attachments, cherished beliefs, and patterns of behavior.

The contemplations concerned with the repulsive nature of the body and with the stages of decomposition are specifically designed to eliminate the perceptual distortion that causes us to view the body as attractive and desirable. As indicated in the discussion concerning the hindrances, these contemplations also help to remove the hindrance of sense desire when it is manifested as lust or as an attachment to the body.

The Repulsive Nature of the Body

The reflection on the repulsive nature of the body is also referred to as the contemplation on the thirty-two parts of the body. The term *repulsive nature* needs to be clearly understood since experiencing aversion toward the body would indicate that our meditation practice was off course. There is nothing inherently ugly about or wrong with the body; it is not something to be despised. On the contrary, we need to treat it with respect and care. The word *repulsive* is used merely to indicate that there are some aspects of the body that are difficult to see when we are blinded by passion and sense desire.

When we think about someone's beautiful hair, for example, we rarely consider what their hair looks like when it is dirty, or how we would react if we found a strand of their hair in our food. When we see a beautiful smile, we do not consider how the mouth smells when the teeth are not brushed or what the teeth look like when they are seen outside of a person's mouth. When we think about the skin, we do not reflect on what happens when the skin ages or about the odor that comes from the body when it is unwashed. When we think about the body itself, we do not consider what it looks like beneath the surface of the skin with the presence of bones, organs, blood, pus, urine, and feces.

To conduct this contemplation, we begin by memorizing the names of the thirty-two parts of the body, as listed in the sutta (see table 4, on the following page). We then reflect on the color, shape, possible odor, origin, and location of each part. Reflecting on the origin means considering how each part of the body arises from the food we eat and is comprised of blood, waste products, and various other elements. We can study anatomy charts or even arrange to view an autopsy to gain an accurate picture of the body parts. The next step is to visualize each body part as it may appear within our own body, in an attempt to recognize its true nature, unobstructed by passion or sense desire.

Finally, we focus on the body part that is clearest to us, and continue concentrating on this object, as we did on the breath, until jhana is achieved. As with mindfulness of breathing, one then turns this contemplation into a vehicle for insight by reflecting on the impermanent nature of the jhanic factors, or by reflecting on the impermanence of the part of the body that was used to achieve the jhana.

The Stages of Decomposition

Meditation on the stages of decomposition is also known as "the nine cemetery contemplations." In years past, meditators in India and other Asian countries were able to visit cemeteries to view bodies as they were undergoing the various stages of decomposition. The contemplation was conducted to help develop a non-attached attitude toward the physical form. There is a critical distinction between a "detached" and a "non-attached" perspective. Detachment, the opposite of attachment, necessarily involves the pushing away or rejection of something that is being experienced. Non-attachment, on the other hand, is observing what is occurring with equanimity. It is being present without attempting to cling to or resist an experience. Developing a non-attached

TABLE 4

THE THIRTY-TWO PARTS OF THE BODY

1. Hair on the head	17. Stomach
2. Hair on the body	18. Undigested food
3. Nails	19. Feces
4. Teeth	20. Brain
5. Skin	21. Bile
6. Flesh	22. Phlegm
7. Sinews	23. Pus
8. Bones	24. Blood
9. Marrow	25. Sweat
10. Kidneys	26. Fat
11. Heart	27. Tears
12. Liver	28. Lymph
13. Intestines	29. Saliva
14. Spleen	30. Nasal mucus
15. Lungs	31. Oil of the joints
16. Bowels	32. Urine

attitude toward the body is achieved through recognizing the body's impermanent and selfless nature.

In this country, we hide the process of decomposition by embalming those who have died and applying makeup to their faces. This makes it quite difficult to see the stages of decomposition as they actually take place. However, the Buddha's graphic descriptions of the process of decomposition enable us to visualize the various stages of decay and to see the body for what it really is.

The following are the stages of decay described by the Buddha and detailed in the commentaries:

1. The body swells up.

2. The body turns shades of red in places where flesh is prominent, turns white in places where pus has collected, and turns blue-black everywhere else.

3. Pus flows from the broken parts of the skin and from the other openings in the body.

4. The skin, flesh, and organs are devoured by animals, flies, and maggots.

5. The body is reduced to a skeleton held together by the tendons with flesh and blood adhering to them.

6. The skeleton is blood-smeared and held together by tendons but without flesh.

7. The bones are scattered in all directions after the tendons wither.

8. The bones begin to disintegrate.

9. The bones turn to dust and blow away.

According to the Buddha's instructions, as we contemplate the various stages of decomposition, we are to reflect that "Truly this body too has the same nature; it will become like that body and will not go beyond that nature." As difficult as this contemplation may be, it is very effective in helping to dislodge the perspective of a compact, beautiful, and permanent body.

The Postures of the Body

As we engage in various activities throughout the day, the body primarily assumes one of four postures: walking, standing, sitting, or lying down. The body also makes smaller movements, such as bending, stretching, raising the hand, turning the head, and so on, while in each of the four main positions. This present contemplation is concerned with "knowing," or being mindfully aware of what is taking place within the body and mind both prior to and at the time the body assumes each of its postures. There are several levels to this awareness.

The first level of awareness is realizing what the body is doing while it is engaged in each activity. Although most of us would say that we are aware, for example, that we are walking when we are walking, our minds are most likely focused on something other than the act of walking. We may be thinking about dinner, about an issue we want to resolve, or about a particular person we are going to meet. This is a lack of being truly present as we engage in various activities taking place throughout the day.

A formal practice that supports the development of our moment-to-moment awareness while assuming different postures is walking meditation. To practice walking meditation, find a straight and level walkway that continues for approximately twenty-five feet. This path length avoids the difficulty of having to stop frequently to turn around. A longer path would not be suitable since without the need to stop occasionally, the mind tends to lose its focus.

Each step in walking meditation is performed in slow motion. As with sitting meditation, you cultivate momentary concentration, apply the principles of bare attention, and observe the three characteristics of experience.

Begin with both feet touching the floor and with your hands hanging at your sides (figure 7). Stay in this posture for about one minute, until your attention is focused on the rise and fall of your breath and you feel centered. Slowly raise your hands and place the palm of one hand on your abdomen and the palm of the other hand on top of the first (figure 8). The hand that is placed on top is not important. Look down at the ground at a point about three feet in front of you. Your mouth is closed and you are breathing through your nose.

You are going to coordinate the stages of the walking process with the natural flow of your in-breath and out-breath. Begin by slowly raising the heel of your right foot (figure 9) and coordinating this movement with your inhalation. After the right heel

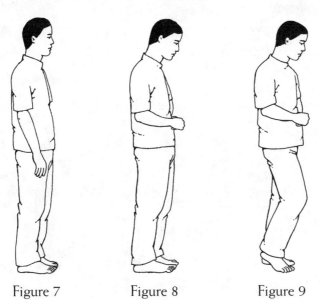

Figure 7　　　　Figure 8　　　　Figure 9

is lifted (with your toes still touching the ground), maintain this posture and exhale slowly. Raise your right foot off the floor and shift it forward (figure 10) while slowly inhaling. Drop your right foot to the floor (figure 11) while slowly exhaling.

As you begin lifting the heel of your left foot, coordinating it with your inhalation, move your body slightly forward to maintain your balance (figure 12). After the left heel is lifted (with your toes still touching the ground), maintain this posture and exhale slowly. Raise your left foot off the floor and shift it forward a short distance beyond your right foot (figure 13), and slowly inhale. Drop your left foot to the floor (figure 14) while slowly exhaling.

Continue with these slow walking movements until you reach the end of the walkway. Stop when you reach the end of the walkway and drop your hands to your sides. Stay in this posture for a short while until your concentration is once again centered on the rise and fall of your breath.

Raise your hands, placing them on your abdomen as you did before, and begin turning around. Coordinate the turning

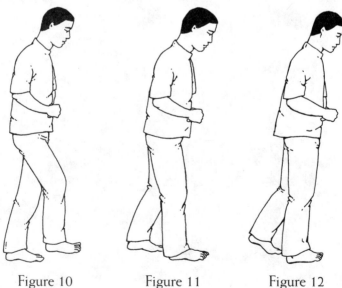

Figure 10   Figure 11   Figure 12

movements with your breathing as you did for walking. Repeat the sequence of steps until the turn is completed. When you complete your turn and are facing the length of the path once again, drop your hands to your sides. Keep repeating the sequence of walking and turning for the duration of the meditation session.

While coordinating your breath with your physical movements, remember to pay bare attention to what is taking place; let go of judgments, decisions, or comments regarding the walking process or what you are noticing as you continue to walk. Observe the impermanent nature of the sensations involved with your walking experience. Bring attention to your legs and feet, experiencing the rise and fall of the sensations that occur from moment to moment. When your mind shifts to another object of awareness, focus on seeing that it is also impermanent. Then, gently but firmly, place your attention back on the sensations associated with your walking movements, while keeping these movements gently coordinated with your breath.

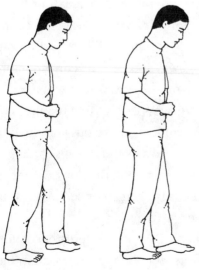

Figure 13   Figure 14

A second level of awareness regarding the postures of the body is the realization that before we move into any position, there is always an intention to do so. We need to directly experience that the intention and the movement of the body are two distinct events, one mental and one physical.

This process can be explained in physiological terms. The intention to walk generates a form of mental energy. This energy is discharged through the nervous system. The nervous system creates muscle impulses, and by virtue of these impulses the physical act of walking takes place. The moment we stop creating the intention to walk, the movement stops.

To directly observe the relationship between intention and movement, keep focusing on the physical sensations involved in the process of standing, walking, and turning (while still gently coordinating each movement with the breath). Become intimate with the rising and falling sensations in the legs and feet. Focus on whichever sensation is strongest.

By paying very close attention to the beginning of each movement and to the rising stage of each sensation associated with that movement, the mind's role in creating the movement—its impulse or intention—will eventually become evident. If we become clearly aware of the ending of each movement and the falling-away stage of the corresponding sensations, the intention to stop the movement will also become clear. Note that even the process of standing requires constant intention. If we were to become unconscious and the intention to stand were to cease, the body would collapse.

A third level of knowing regarding the postures of the body is the awareness that there is no person or self behind the postures or movements. When we are not aware of the interdependent process of intention and the movement that follows, we may believe that walking and the other postures are initiated by a permanent self. By practicing walking meditation we eventually realize that the intention and the corresponding movement that arises in one moment does not continue into the very next moment. It will become quite apparent that in every moment a new mind and body arises and falls away. We directly observe that there is no self who is doing the walking. It is merely a conditioned process.

Clear Comprehension

Clear comprehension refers to the precise, complete, and balanced knowing of what is truly occurring during each moment of our experience. Precise knowing is recognizing the separate but interdependent aspects of the body and mind as we are engaged in each of our activities. Complete knowing is realizing the more profound characteristics of the sensory experiences we encounter—that they are impermanent, unsatisfactory, and selfless. Balanced knowing is observing each of our activities with mindfulness so that our mental factors work in harmony and provide a true picture of what is actually taking place.

Clear comprehension can support the arising of insight when we are not engaged in sitting or walking meditation. Within the scope of clear comprehension, the Buddha includes activities such as going forward or backward; looking ahead or looking behind; bending or stretching; carrying objects; eating, drinking, chewing, or savoring; answering the calls of nature; falling asleep or waking up; and speaking or remaining silent. In other words, each of our activities falls under the umbrella of "clear comprehension."

There are four facets to clear comprehension: clear comprehension of purpose, clear comprehension of suitability, clear comprehension of the domain of meditation, and clear comprehension of nondelusion.

Clear comprehension of purpose is the recognition of our intention or motivation for engaging in any activity. We need to be certain that our motivations support our spiritual development and do not detract from it. To practice clear comprehension of purpose, we pause before we begin a new activity to determine whether our intended thoughts, words, or deeds will bring us closer to our spiritual goal. If we discover that our intention to think, speak, or act is motivated by greed, hatred, or delusion, we allow that intention to rise and fall without acting upon it. If, on the other hand, we discover that our intention is motivated by generosity, loving-kindness, or wisdom, we pursue that particular activity. It is the process of paying bare attention that gives us the "psychological space," so to speak, to consider the intentions behind our proposed behaviors at a stage prior to the arising of justifications and rationalizations. Without paying bare attention to our intentions, these types of secondary considerations might convince us to engage in activities that would lead us spiritually astray.

Clear comprehension of suitability involves reflecting upon the appropriateness of each intended activity. Although we may aspire toward wholesome spiritual goals, we still need to consider whether our intended activities are in harmony with our current set of circumstances. For example, we may want to begin meditating, but one of our family members needs our attention. If we ignore considerations of time and place, and attempt to superimpose our agenda over situational limitations, we set ourselves up for frustration and failure.

Clear comprehension of the domain of meditation refers to extending the range or scope of our mindful awareness into every nook and cranny of our lives. It means approaching each activity with the question, "How can I use this present moment to further my spiritual awakening?" Unless we work to penetrate every aspect of our lives with the light of awareness, there will be areas that will remain hidden in darkness even after years of practicing the traditional forms of meditation. These areas may include our eating habits, sexual behaviors, fantasies, and so forth. We may be using these dark areas to avoid dealing with our issues or to find ways to escape from our everyday problems.

Clear comprehension of nondelusion involves recognizing the true nature of our moment-to-moment experience. Of all our distorted views, the most difficult to eradicate is the belief in a permanent self. Clear comprehension of nondelusion works to eliminate this deep-seated misperception and replace it with the realization of selflessness.

The Four Material Elements

The view expressed in the *Visuddhimagga* is that the body, and every other form of matter, is composed of four elements: earth, water, fire, and air.

The earth element has the characteristics of solidity and stiffness. We are experiencing the earth element when we feel the hardness or softness of sense objects. Earth is the primary element present in the body's bones, organs, nails, and teeth.

The water element has the characteristic of liquidity and has the nature to flow. Water has the ability to bind things together, for instance, when water combines with flour resulting in dough. The water element is experienced as heaviness. Water is the primary element present in tears, sweat, saliva, blood, and urine.

The fire element has the characteristic of temperature. It is experienced as heat in the body. It is responsible for the aging of the body and for the process of digestion. The fire element can manifest as lightness, as seen in the rising of hot air.

The air element has the characteristic of expansion, which can be observed, for instance, when a balloon expands as air is pumped into it. The air element is responsible for motion. It manifests in the body as the breath, the force that creates belching or hiccupping, and as the gas we feel in the stomach and intestines.

We may designate something as primarily associated with one element because of the predominance of that element in our experience of that object. However, all four elements can be found in every object that exists in the sensory world. When we dive into the water and land on our chest and stomach, for example, we feel the earth element that is present in water. When we burn wood and beads of moisture appear on the wood, it reveals the presence of the water element in earth. When we get a mosquito bite, the resulting burning sensation is the experience of the fire element.

The purpose of contemplation of the four material elements is to recognize the manner in which each element manifests in the body and thereby further dispel the perception that the body is an entity that endures through time. We can use the process of walking meditation to experience the presence of the four elements and to see how they change from one moment to the next.

As you raise the heel of the foot, you feel a sensation of lightness, an aspect of the fire element. As the toes are pressed against the ground you encounter resistance, which is a manifestation of the earth element. As you raise the foot in the air, you again observe the fire element. When you move the foot forward, the movement is an aspect of the air element. When you put the foot down, its heaviness is the experience of the water element. When you transfer weight to the foot you have just put down, the earth element is again predominant.

Using walking meditation as a way to experience the elements weakens the perception that the body is a solid or permanent entity that contains a substantial self. An analogy in the *Mahasatipatthana Sutta* explains how the meditation on the four elements works. When a butcher takes his cow to be slaughtered, he considers that it is a cow he is leading to the slaughterhouse. When he is butchering the cow, he thinks that it is a cow that is being butchered. However, when he packages the meat and sells it by the side of a road, he no longer thinks that it is a cow he is selling, but simply pieces of meat. The perception of a cow has dissolved because the individual parts have been clearly seen. Similarly, when we are engaged in daily activities, we consider that it is a body that is participating in those activities. However, as we engage in this meditation process, the perception of a body begins to dissolve. We no longer feel it is a body that is experiencing these activities, but that it is simply the rising and falling of the four elements according to particular causes and conditions. With the contemplation on the four elements, the section on the mindfulness of the body has been completed.

MINDFULNESS OF FEELINGS

When we practice mindfulness of feelings, we shift our focus from noticing the impermanent, conditioned, and selfless nature of the body to identifying these same three characteristics as attributes of the mind and mental objects. As we begin to investigate feelings, the interdependence of the mind and body becomes evident.

In the same way that we isolated the body from all other objects of consciousness when we began the body contemplations, it is essential to remain mindful of "the feelings in the feelings." We need to avoid dwelling on any judgments, decisions, or internal commentary that may arise based upon the feelings we are observing. We must be careful not to identify with the feelings and consider them "ours." We simply maintain a mindful awareness of each feeling as it presents itself to consciousness from moment to moment.

We began exploring the aggregate of feelings in the chapter concerned with purification of virtue. We described how a feeling automatically arises whenever a sensory experience occurs. A feeling in this context is not an emotion, but rather the direct experience of a sense object as being pleasant, unpleasant, or neither pleasant nor unpleasant.

The Buddha further describes feelings by dividing them into three pairs. The first pair contains pleasant worldly feelings and pleasant spiritual feelings. A pleasant worldly feeling arises when we have contact with a pleasant sense object, or when we think about an aspect of worldly life that brings us pleasure (thoughts of family, friends, personal interests, and so on). A pleasant spiritual feeling arises in connection with meditation practice, such as when we experience the joy associated with deep concentration, when we have a spiritual insight, and so forth.

The second pair includes unpleasant worldly feelings and unpleasant spiritual feelings. An unpleasant worldly feeling arises when we have contact with an unpleasant sense object or when we think about an aspect of worldly life that brings us psychological pain (thoughts of losing a family member, failing at some task, losing a job, and so forth). An unpleasant spiritual feeling arises in connection with meditation practice. We may experience disappointment, for example, when our spiritual progress is slower than we thought it would be, or we may experience fear when we realize just how impermanent everything really is.

The final pair of feelings consists of neutral worldly feelings and neutral spiritual feelings. A neutral worldly feeling is a feeling of indifference. It arises when we have contact with a worldly sense object that neither brings us pleasure nor pain, or when we give consideration to an aspect of worldly life that holds no interest for us. This feeling may arise, for example, when we see the same billboard on the way to work each day, or when we hear a weather report for a place we have no plans on visiting. A neutral spiritual feeling, however, is experienced as equanimity and is the result of spiritual maturity. A mind possessing the quality of equanimity experiences every object of consciousness without attachment or aversion. It develops naturally as we proceed with our practice of meditation and continue to observe things as they are.

Although feelings automatically arise whenever there is sense contact, the type of feeling that we experience can be influenced by our perception of the sense object being experienced. For example, hearing someone sing while we are listening to the radio may result in a pleasant feeling, but hearing someone sing when we are trying to meditate may result in an unpleasant feeling. Recognizing that we cannot control everyone or everything in our life may create an unpleasant feeling, but realizing that there is no self to be in control can result in a feeling of equanimity.

If we are not aware of the feelings as they rise and fall from moment to moment—if we are not guarding the sense doors— we may either react to the feelings we experience or to the objects upon which the feelings are based. The tendency is to grasp at pleasant feelings or objects, to resist unpleasant feelings or objects, and to become bored with or indifferent toward feelings and objects that are neither pleasant nor unpleasant. This reactivity is part of a conditioned chain of events that occurs without the necessity of a self driving the process.

The following contemplations support the arising of insight into the nature of feelings, the ways in which we react to those feelings, and the impersonal causes and conditions behind the feelings themselves. The contemplation of feelings plays a key role in helping to break the chain that keeps us in bondage to our sensory experiences.

For the first exercise, choose any one of the sense organs to work with for an entire day. Observe the particular feelings that occur when sense objects are encountered through that sense door. When feelings occur, their presence may be experienced as bodily sensations or merely intuited without having specifically located them in the body. However, it is essential to directly experience the feelings and not just to theorize that they must have occurred. Determine whether each feeling that arises is pleasant, unpleasant, or neutral. In the following days, repeat this process for each of the other sense organs. Remember that the mind is considered a sense organ that experiences thoughts, feelings, volitions, and other mental formations as its sense objects.

The first contemplation enables us to recognize how feelings arise spontaneously when sense contact occurs. It reveals how feelings are conditioned by those contacts, and how we have no choice as to whether feelings will arise. It also helps us recognize just how incessantly consciousness is being impinged upon by feelings.

To practice the second exercise, we continue to meditate by focusing on the rise and fall of every in-breath and every out-breath, noticing with great precision their impermanent nature. Whenever the mind shifts its attention to another object of awareness, we recognize the impermanent nature of that object, and then gently but firmly return to the breath. If at any point, however, we realize that we have lost our focus for an extended period of time, we immediately reflect back to see what initially distracted the mind's attention. We may find that it was not the thoughts, images, or sense objects themselves that we were reacting to, but to the feelings that were associated with those experiences.

The second contemplation illuminates the conditioned nature of the mind and the way in which the mind reacts to feelings without any conscious consideration on our part. It enables us to discover how the mind grasps after pleasant feelings or the objects that provide those feelings, how it resists unpleasant feelings or objects, and how it becomes bored or indifferent with feelings or objects that are neutral. As a result of this contemplation we realize that the mind's reactivity to sensory experience is conditioned, dependently arisen, and occurs without a self in control of the process.

In the final exercise, we use feelings as an opportunity to discover the true nature of our moment-to-moment experience. This contemplation, if diligently practiced, will lead to significant insights.

After sitting in meditation for an extended period of time, bodily pain begins to arise. The first strategy is to watch the rise and fall of the painful feeling and then to return to our breath. However, if the feeling is very intense, we will find it difficult to stay focused on the breath. When this occurs, we begin using the painful feeling as the primary object of our meditation.

The typical response to an unpleasant feeling is to resist it or to engage in some activity that may change the nature of the feeling we are experiencing. In terms of sitting meditation, we may decide to change positions or to slightly adjust our posture. By doing so, however, we lose our concentration and are not following one of the most important principles of insight meditation: to remain choicelessly aware of whatever arises to consciousness. The issue with pain, more than the unpleasant feeling itself, is the fear of being overwhelmed by the experience. As a result, we tend to mentally and physically tighten around pain when it occurs. This response serves to intensify the unpleasant experience.

To practice this contemplation, we are to relax, soften, and settle into the experience of the painful feeling. We are to become so intimate with the pain that we can penetrate our misperceptions about the unpleasant feeling and see it for what it really is. We will then be able to recognize the impermanent nature of the pain and discover that there is no pain in the knee, back, or other location as such. The place in which we feel the pain actually keeps shifting from moment to moment. Further, if we are very attentive, we realize that between pulsations of pain, there is the absence of pain.

We will also find that the quality of pain keeps changing. We may first experience the sensation as burning, then as pressure, then as throbbing, and so forth. If we are able to remain fully present with the pain, it often reaches a point where it breaks up and completely disappears, showing once again its impermanence.

By remaining present with the experience, we will also become aware of the unsatisfactory nature of feelings. Of course, with painful feelings this is quite obvious. However, if we were to remain choicelessly present with the most pleasurable of feelings, we would eventually see them change into unpleasant feelings. This makes all feelings, even pleasant ones, impermanent and ultimately unsatisfactory.

As we continue to observe the painful feelings, we discover their selfless nature. We realize that what is actually occurring is the rise and fall of unpleasant feelings, concurrent with the rise and fall of the awareness, or consciousness, of those feelings. There is no self as part of, behind, or in control of the process. The feelings arise due to sense contact, and in effect, the feeling itself is the feeler. When this insight occurs, we discover the difference between a feeling and the mind's aversive reaction to that feeling. This insight transforms our relationship to feelings, enabling us to maintain our equanimity with whatever feelings arise.

KNOWLEDGE OF CONDITIONALITY

When we have no direct experience of the specific causes and conditions responsible for the arising of the five aggregates and the way in which they maintain a continuity without the presence of a self, we tend to form speculative views about the process we call life. We may wonder if we existed in the past, if we truly exist now, or if we will exist at some point in the future. We may believe that a creator-deity initiated and continues to preserve life, or that life is a chance occurrence that ends with the death of the body.

By practicing insight meditation according to the instructions given in the *Mahasatipatthana Sutta*, we begin to cultivate knowledge of conditionality, which is realizing the dependently arisen nature of the five aggregates. We begin to comprehend how the five aggregates can be impermanent and selfless, while still seeming to maintain continuity from moment to moment.

By following the body contemplations we discover that the body is not a solid entity, but is a conglomeration of many parts. We realize that the functioning of the body can be experienced as an expression of earth, water, fire, and air. We begin to recognize that the body is selfless and that it moves in response to dependently arisen intentionality, which originates within the mind.

As a result of practicing mindfulness of feelings, we discover that feelings arise dependent upon sense contact. We realize that the mind reacts to the presence of pleasant, unpleasant, and neutral feelings due to its prior conditioning. By examining the feelings that arise to consciousness, we discern their impermanent, unsatisfactory, and selfless nature.

Examining the body and feelings provides initial insights into the causes and conditions responsible for our moment-to-moment experience. These insights counter previously held views that our experience is under the control of an independent self or is being overseen by some outside force. The next stage of purification, purification by knowledge and vision of what is the path and what is not the path, penetrates even more deeply into the conditioned nature of all experience.

OF WHAT IS THE PATH AND WHAT IS NOT THE PATH

As we continue our practice of insight meditation and our knowledge of conditionality comes to maturity, we reach a new stage in our spiritual development. At this point, two additional insight knowledges begin to emerge: knowledge by comprehension and knowledge of arising and passing away.

Knowledge by comprehension is the continued recognition that each moment of consciousness, along with its corresponding object, is impermanent, unsatisfactory, and selfless. We have already been observing these three characteristics, which are inherent to all phenomena, but our ability to identify their presence now encompasses a wider scope of objects and reaches a more profound level of development.

The knowledge of arising and passing away, the next knowledge to unfold, has two specific phases. The initial phase occurs as part of the purification by knowledge and vision of what is the path and what is not the path, and will eventually come to maturity during the next stage of spiritual development, the purification by knowledge and vision of the way. During the initial phase of the knowledge of arising and passing away, the realization that every aspect of our experience appears and disappears according to specific causes and conditions deeply impresses itself upon the mind. Although we have already been examining the conditioned nature of our experience, at this point, we are able to view the process with a clarity not previously available to us.

As these knowledges continue to unfold, we begin to experience some of the more profound benefits of insight meditation. The deep meaning of statements spoken by the Buddha, or by our spiritual mentors, may become completely clear. A profound sense of happiness and calm may be realized. An overwhelming enthusiasm for continuing the practice may arise along with a desire to live in a meditation center. The ability to stay mindfully present with whatever arises from moment to moment may become effortless.

The arising of these knowledges, insights, and experiences is an indication that our practice is maturing. However, these same experiences can become a barrier to further spiritual development. This occurs when we identify with the experiences, become attached to them, or believe that they are signs that we have become enlightened. If identification, attachment, or belief occurs, we are off the path, and the experiences are regarded as corruptions of insight. When we begin to realize, either through self-discovery or as a result of working with a teacher, that we have been grasping at these experiences and have not been treating them as impermanent objects of awareness, the understanding places us back on the true path. When this occurs, we have reached the stage of development referred to as the purification by knowledge and vision of what is the path and what is not the path. Practicing the contemplations associated with mindfulness of consciousness and mindfulness of dhammas, as they are described in the *Mahasatipatthana Sutta*, supports our efforts to reach this present stage of spiritual purification.

MINDFULNESS OF CONSCIOUSNESS

Most of us tend to identify with consciousness more than with any of the other five aggregates. While we can usually gain some measure of objectivity regarding the body and mental formations, we typically believe that it is our self that is conscious or aware of what is occurring from moment to moment.

Consciousness is merely the awareness of each sense object as it presents itself to one of the six sense doors. There is no self that is conscious, and there is no state of consciousness that endures through time. Consciousness is actually a continuum of momentary acts of awareness that rise and fall along with their respective objects due to specific causes and conditions.

Whenever a sense object impinges on a specific sense organ, consciousness illuminates the corresponding sense field (the visual field, the auditory field, the cognitive field, and so forth). It does so without any interpretation, modification, or attempt to control the sensory experience in any way. Consciousness acts as a type of motion detector, which, when triggered, simply illuminates any objects that have come within its range.

Although consciousness does not interact with that which it illuminates, when consciousness arises it does so in conjunction with certain mental factors. These mental factors perform specific tasks in regard to the sense object that consciousness is focused upon. For example, feeling is the experience of a sense object as pleasant, unpleasant, or neutral; perception, working in conjunction with memory, recognizes the distinctive marks of a sense object; volition decides what will occur in regard to the sense object; and so forth.

Each moment of consciousness can be classified according to the mental factors with which it is associated. From the standpoint of reaching the deeper stages of purification, the most important classification of consciousness is that associated with volition, since it determines whether our momentary acts of consciousness are skillful and wholesome, or unskillful and thus unwholesome. Both skillful and unskillful states of mind are considered to be the "roots" of actions, since all behaviors originate from or are rooted in these states. The three unskillful roots are: greed, which can manifest as attachment, craving, or desire; hatred, which can appear as aversion, anger, or ill will; and delusion, which emerges as spiritual blindness, confusion, or ignorance. When any unskillful root is present, so is delusion. The three skillful roots are generosity, loving-kindness, and wisdom or spiritual understanding.

If unskillful states are allowed to run unimpeded through the mind, the thoughts, words, and deeds we commit from those mind states will result in circumstances that will hinder our spiritual progress. On the other hand, if we cultivate skillful states of mind, our thoughts, words, and deeds will result in circumstances that will support the arising of more advanced stages of spiritual development. The following two exercises promote the development of skillful states of mind and will generate insight into the true nature of consciousness.

In the first contemplation, we identify whether each state of mind that arises is skillful or unskillful. Begin by focusing on the breath as the primary object of meditation. Whenever the mind becomes distracted and attention wanders, immediately focus on the new object of awareness to determine the specific quality of consciousness that has just arisen.

For example, if we begin thinking of a family member and we yearn to see that person, if we start reflecting on what will be served for dinner, or if we find that we are fantasizing about a sexual encounter, we should recognize these states of mind as rooted in greed. If we replay a recent argument and feel angry, if we dwell on memories of past grievances, or if we experience fear regarding what the future may bring, we should identify these states of mind as rooted in hatred. If we are doubting that any progress will be made through the practice of meditation, if the mind is restless and cannot stay with the object of meditation, if we are confused and cannot decide how to align our life with spiritual values, we should know that these are states of mind rooted in delusion.

If thoughts of supporting a meditation center arise, if we think about sharing the Dhamma with others, or if we consider how to simplify our life, we recognize these states of mind as being rooted in generosity. If we have loving thoughts of gratitude for the teachings we have received, if compassion arises for those who are suffering, or if we are feeling joy for those who have made progress through their meditation practice, we should understand that these states of mind are rooted in loving-kindness. If the mind is able to recognize the three characteristics of experience, if we feel great confidence in the teachings, or if the mind is calm and clear, we should recognize that these states are rooted in nondelusion and wisdom. Remember to observe what is occurring without judgment, decision, or commentary. We are merely noticing the presence of skillful and unskillful states of mind.

By performing this contemplation we accomplish two things. First, we become aware of our skillful and unskillful states of mind and see how these states lead to our behaviors and, ultimately, to the mundane and spiritual circumstances in which we find ourselves. Secondly, the moments of mindful awareness that actually enable us to recognize our states of mind are themselves skillful, and they work to create behaviors and circumstances conducive to our spiritual development.

As we discussed, consciousness can only have one object at a time. When mindfulness, a skillful state of mind, uncovers the presence of an unskillful state, that particular state no longer exists. In the same way that a boat moving through the water leaves a wake, whatever experience passes through the mind also leaves a wake or impression in the mind. Mindfulness recognizes the presence of the impression left by the unskillful state. Therefore, through the application of mindfulness we are turning unskillful states of mind into skillful ones.

In the second contemplation, consciousness itself is taken as the primary object of attention. The goal is to directly realize that consciousness is impermanent, unsatisfactory, and selfless. For this exercise, it is not necessary to recognize whether any state of mind is skillful or unskillful.

We begin by following the breath. When we become aware that our attention has moved to another object of awareness, we immediately reflect back to observe that not only is the breath no longer the object of our awareness, but the moment of consciousness that was noticing the breath has also disappeared. What is actually present at this time is a moment of consciousness that is taking the memory of the previous moment of consciousness as its object. In other words, to conduct this contemplation we keep using our current moments of consciousness to realize that the prior moments of consciousness, along with their objects, have totally vanished.

If we work diligently with this exercise, we will directly experience the lightning speed with which consciousness and its object arise and pass away. We will further recognize how this impermanent process is beyond our control and is, therefore, an unsatisfactory experience. Finally, we will discover that each act of consciousness is conditioned, and that it rises and falls from moment to moment without a self behind, in control of, or as part of the process. This insight translates into the recognition that there is no "one" who is conscious or aware.

MINDFULNESS OF DHAMMAS

Dhamma is one of the most important terms in the Buddhist lexicon. It is used to indicate the natural law of the universe; the teachings of the Buddha; the various objects of consciousness; and in its most expanded meaning, everything that exists. It is in this last sense that the word *dhamma* is currently being used.

In the mindfulness of dhammas section of the *Mahasatipatthana Sutta*, five categories of dhammas are discussed: the five hindrances (which we have already discussed), the five aggregates, the six internal and six external sense bases, the seven factors of enlightenment, and the Four Noble Truths. We will explore the latter four categories in turn and suggest specific contemplations to support our understanding of the dhammas that correspond to each category. Since we addressed the five hindrances when we discussed the purification of view, we will begin our review of dhammas with the five aggregates of clinging.

The Five Aggregates of Clinging

The five aggregates are material form, feelings, perceptions, mental formations, and consciousness. Material form refers to the physical body and all other forms of matter in the universe. All matter exhibits the characteristics of the four primary elements: earth, water, fire, and air. The other four aggregates encompass the mental aspect of our experience.

Feeling is the experience of a sense object as being pleasant, unpleasant, or neutral. A sensation that occurs in the body is physical, or an aspect of material form, but the feeling that arises based upon that sensation is mental. Perception identifies the distinctive marks of an object and is closely associated with the faculty of memory. Perception enables the mind to recognize forms, sounds, tastes, and so on. Mental formations are the mental factors, such as thoughts and emotions, that arise in conjunction with consciousness. Volition or intention is a key mental formation that forms the basis of *kamma*, the law of cause and effect. Feelings and perceptions are also mental formations, which the Buddha considered significant enough to discuss separately. The fifth aggregate is consciousness, which is the pure and selfless moment-to-moment awareness of a sense object.

We tenaciously cling to the view that a self exists relative to these five aggregates, which is why they are referred to as the five aggregates of clinging. The Buddha isolated twenty potential views of self. He specified four possible perspectives we may have in relation to each of the five aggregates; these perspectives comprise the twenty views.

The first perspective is that we are actually one of the five aggregates: that we are the body, we are the feelings, we are the one that perceives or makes distinctions, we are the thoughts that are conceived, or we are that which is conscious of everything that is experienced. The second view is that although we are not one of the aggregates, there is a self or soul that exists outside of the five aggregates and is in control of them. The third view is that our self is contained somewhere within the five aggregates—for example, in the brain or in consciousness. The final view is that our self is some huge universal entity that contains the five aggregates: we are one with the Atman, God, or Universal Consciousness, and the aggregates appear as our manifestation. (In this last view there is still a belief in the existence of an independent self considered part of everything else.)

However, when we thoroughly investigate our experiences, we discover no self as part of, in control of, within, or beyond the five aggregates. We see nothing more than these five aggregates operating interdependently, rising and falling from moment to moment due to specific causes and conditions. The exercises that follow are designed to eliminate the false views of self and to enable us to recognize our experiences for what they really are.

For the first contemplation, we thoroughly investigate each of our experiences throughout the day to discover that they are nothing more than manifestations of the five aggregates. We do this by first observing and then labeling whatever arises. We identify the breath or the corresponding tactile sensation, for example, as being material form. When a feeling arises, we classify it as a manifestation of the feeling aggregate. When the mind recognizes a sense object, we realize that a perception has arisen. When there is intention to act, we label it as a volition or mental formation. When we experience a sense object, we recognize the awareness of the object to be the aggregate of consciousness. We continue to perform this contemplation until it becomes clear to us that each and every one of our experiences can be accounted for within the framework of the five aggregates.

The second exercise builds upon the first. We made reference to this contemplation in the last chapter when we discussed the clear comprehension of nondelusion. For this contemplation, whenever you are about to engage in an activity, stop and ask yourself, "Who is about to engage in this activity?" Follow this question with an immediate investigation of the conditioned, dependently arisen, and selfless nature of what is actually taking place.

When you realize that you intend to eat, for example, stop and ask yourself, "Who is about to eat?" Now investigate what is truly occurring. It was not you or a self that made the decision to eat; it was the five aggregates acting interdependently. First there was an unpleasant physical sensation or feeling in the body. The mind compared the feeling with the memory of similar sensations, and the aggregate of perception named the feeling "hunger." A thought arose to consciousness that to alleviate that unpleasant sensation, food was needed. As a result, the intention to eat arose. Finally, consciousness was aware of what was occurring throughout the entire process. In sum, the intention to eat was conditioned by the unpleasant feelings of hunger. There was no self that made an independent decision to eat.

As a second example, after finishing your meal, your children begin to argue. Your requests for them to calm down go unheeded, and you feel anger begin to arise. At that point you stop and ask yourself, "Who is getting angry?" Examine the experience of becoming angry. Recognize that the sounds you heard were perceived to be "arguing." Based upon that perception, thoughts or mental formations arose that may have said, "Why must they always argue? Why can't I just relax after my meal without having to deal with this? Won't they ever learn? What's wrong with them?" and so forth. Notice that the body became tense (the earth element), the breath quickened (the air element), and the face felt warm (the fire element), all of which are unpleasant feelings. The intention or volition to end the argument subsequently came to the surface of the mind. Throughout the process, consciousness was aware of each arising of materiality, feeling, perception, and mental formation.

In other words, the arising of anger was nothing more than the conditioned mind reacting to stimuli perceived as being unpleasant. There was no independent, angry self within the five aggregates. It was actually our identification with the thoughts, perceptions, sensations, and moments of consciousness that created the illusion that "I" was angry.

It is important to remember that these are not theoretical exercises, but direct investigations of our experience. These contemplations are quite powerful and support the arising of profound spiritual insights.

The Six Internal and Six External Sense Bases

The twelve sense bases, six internal and six external, describe the same world of experience as the five aggregates of clinging, but from a different perspective. The six internal sense bases are the six sense organs, and the six external sense bases are their corresponding objects. The eye sees forms; the ear hears sounds; the nose smells odors; the tongue experiences tastes; the body feels tangible objects; and the mind, or consciousness, encounters mental objects, subtle forms of matter, and nibbana—the unconditioned dhamma. When we refer to the internal sense bases, it is not the physical organs themselves that are meant, but the sensitive material within the sense organs that contacts the sense objects. They are called "sense bases" because they function as the basis for the arising of the corresponding type of consciousness (eye consciousness, ear consciousness, and so forth).

The Buddha gives a striking analogy that reveals the source of our attachment to sensory experience. He tells his listeners of a black bull and a white bull joined together by a yoke around their necks. He asks if the black bull is a fetter for the white bull or if the white bull is a fetter for the black bull. He is answered that neither bull is a fetter for the other; it is the yoke around their necks that acts as a fetter, binding the two bulls.

Similarly, the Buddha states that it is not our sense organs that fetter us to sense objects, and it is not sense objects that fetter us to our sense organs. It is actually our greed, hatred, and delusion that fetter the sense organs to their corresponding sense objects. A fully enlightened being has sense organs and experiences sense objects, but is not fettered to them, since all traces of greed, hatred, and delusion have been eradicated. The following contemplation enables us to realize the ways in which greed, hatred, and delusion act as fetters.

During meditation we continue to use the breath as the main object of awareness. When our attention shifts to another sense object, we investigate to determine whether greed, hatred, or delusion arose in relation to that new object. If we recognize the presence of greed, we observe how the mind with greed reaches out through the sense organ and acts to bind, chain, or fetter the mind to that sense object. If we find that resistance to a sense object is present, we want to realize how the mind with hatred or aversion first grasps and becomes bound to the very object that it wants to eliminate. (We cannot attempt to push something away without first coming in contact with it.) Finally, if delusion regarding a sense object arises and we identify with that object as being me or mine, we recognize how the mind with delusion is defined (or fettered) by the very object with which it is identified.

It may come as quite a shock to our mind, which we may have previously considered free, to discover how fettered we are to sensory experiences. This recognition, however, can act as an impetus for us to initiate the causes and conditions that will end this form of bondage and enable us to achieve spiritual liberation.

The Seven Factors of Enlightenment

Enlightenment can be said to occur when the mind reaches the seventh stage of purification and is in accord with the Four Noble Truths. The seven factors of enlightenment (mindfulness, investigation of dhammas, energy or effort, rapture or joy, tranquillity, concentration, and equanimity) are the specific mental factors that support the fulfillment of this essential attainment. The factors of enlightenment unfold in a particular sequence, with the first factor acting as a base upon which the next factor evolves, and so forth. As each subsequent factor arises, the earlier factors continue to operate in a unified manner. The factors of enlightenment have been present in a rudimentary form throughout each stage of purification; however, with the arising of the purification by knowledge and vision of what is and what is not the path, the factors finally gain the power and momentum necessary to lead us to spiritual liberation.

It is important to recognize the presence of the factors of enlightenment so we can bring them to maturity. It is likewise essential to recognize when they are absent so we can initiate the causes and conditions that will support their arising. After we describe each factor of enlightenment, there will be suggestions on how to further their development.

Mindfulness, the first factor of enlightenment, can be described as a specific type of attention that has the capacity to observe what is occurring to us and within us during successive moments of experience. It is referred to as "bare attention" since it notices what is occurring bare of judgment, decision, and commentary. Opposed to making a superficial observation, mindfulness has the characteristic of sinking deeply into each object it observes. This enables the next factor of enlightenment, investigation of dhammas, to effectively perform its function. The objects of mindfulness are the body, feelings, consciousness, and dhammas, which are collectively referred to as the four foundations of mindfulness.

There is no enlightenment factor more basic than mindfulness; thus, we can only cultivate mindfulness through the continual effort to remain mindful. When the mind loses its present-moment focus and we realize that this has occurred, the realization itself is another moment of mindfulness. In this manner, one moment of mindfulness conditions the arising of the next. This continues until mindfulness becomes a mental habit.

An additional way to facilitate the development of mindfulness is to practice the four clear comprehensions, discussed previously (clear comprehension of purpose, of suitability, of the domain of meditation, and of nondelusion). These contemplations support the development of mindfulness in our daily lives. Mindfulness is also fostered by avoiding contact with people who have confused and scattered minds and cultivating relationships with those who are intent on developing mindfulness. It is also helpful to make a strong determination to remain mindful, since our actions always mirror our intentions.

The second factor of enlightenment is the *investigation of dhammas*. This investigation is not a willful act, in which we are trying to arrive at some conclusion. The investigation of dhammas is synonymous with insight or wisdom. It is the intuitive, non-intellectual realization of the true nature of body and mind, which arises with the aid of mindfulness.

In addition to mindfulness, there are other conditions that support the development of this factor of enlightenment. Keeping the faculties balanced is essential. As we previously discussed, energy or effort needs to be balanced with calm and concentration, and faith needs to be balanced with discernment. Mindfulness is the mental factor responsible for maintaining the equilibrium between these factors.

Other suggestions to cultivate the investigation of dhammas include: studying the Buddha's teachings to learn more about the dhammas to be investigated; living in a clean and orderly environment that makes it easier to develop a clean and orderly mind needed for the effective investigation of dhammas; avoiding the company of people who are not seeking Truth; and spending time with individuals who encourage the development of insight. Finally, the investigation of dhammas is supported by making a strong determination to promote the arising of wisdom.

Energy or *effort*, the next factor of enlightenment, is considered to be the basis of all spiritual attainment. Without mental effort, our mind cannot stay focused on its objects so that the mindful investigation of dhammas can occur. Our effort must always be in balance. If there is too much effort, agitation will occur and if there is too little effort, sloth and torpor will arise. We must also cultivate courageous energy: the commitment to remain present with whatever arises to consciousness, without grasping or resisting anything that comes to the fore of the mind.

Reflecting on the benefits of energy helps to further its development. We can consider, for example, that all those who have achieved enlightenment in the past did so through the application of energy. Energy can be aroused by contemplating how rare and precious it is to have met with, and to be able to follow, the Buddha's teachings. We can arouse enthusiasm for our practice by considering the astonishing achievement of the Buddha, the depth of wisdom and compassion his teachings represent, and how the door to liberation has been kept ajar for more than 2,500 years by his dedicated disciples.

To develop energy, it is also helpful to avoid lazy people and to associate with those who are vigorous and put forth the effort to practice meditation. Finally, creating a strong intention to manifest the effort needed to achieve enlightenment supports our capacity to do so.

Rapture or joy, the fourth factor of enlightenment, is one of the five attributes of the first jhana. Rapture is the uplifting experience that occurs when the mind takes a pleasurable interest in the dhammas it investigates. Rapture provides a sense of satisfaction, which refreshes both body and mind and supports the work of cultivating insight. There are five grades of rapture: minor, momentary, showering, uplifting, and pervading. One or more of these grades may be experienced as we continue to work through the stages of purification.

Rapture can be fostered by contemplating the extraordinary qualities of the Buddha, Dhamma, and Sangha. The Buddha, in this context, was a historical individual who realized enlightenment at a time when the path to purification was obscured, and dedicated his entire life to showing others the way to freedom. The Dhamma represents the threefold training of morality, concentration, and wisdom, and the truth to which that training leads. The Sangha are those individuals who have tread the path before us, showing that enlightenment is truly possible, as well as those who tread it with us, taking the same spiritual journey. This deep appreciation for what is referred to as the "Triple Gem" continues to grow as we reap the fruits of our spiritual practice.

Rapture can also arise when we consider our own virtue and the acts of generosity we have previously shown. It can occur by reflecting upon the spiritual progress we have already achieved, seeing that we are on a path that leads to the end of all suffering.

To support the arising of rapture, it is helpful to avoid those who are harsh or crude and to associate with those who demonstrate refinement and restraint. Finally, the intention to cultivate rapture is a further support to its development.

The next factor of enlightenment is *tranquillity*. As the mind continues to take pleasurable interest in its objects of awareness, concentration naturally improves. As a result, a deep sense of peace and contentment arises along with the subsiding of mental agitation and feelings of tiredness or fatigue.

Tranquillity can be cultivated in several ways. It is helpful to have practice conditions conducive to developing a calm mind, such as nourishing and agreeable food, comfortable weather conditions, and a peaceful atmosphere. We must be careful, however, not to fall into the trap of looking for the "ideal" place in which to practice, since it certainly does not exist! Once we find a situation that is generally favorable, we will need to cultivate patience in the face of adverse circumstances, which inevitably arise.

Contemplating kamma, the law of cause and effect, further promotes the arising of tranquillity. We can reflect that our current state of mind is the result of the words, thoughts, and deeds we intentionally committed in the past, and that the degree of calm we will be able to achieve in the future is being influenced by the words, thoughts, and deeds we are intentionally committing in the present. To develop tranquillity, it is helpful to avoid people who are restless and agitated and to associate with those who are calm and peaceful. Finally, a strong intention to create and maintain tranquillity is supportive of its arising.

Concentration is the sixth factor of enlightenment. It manifests as the ability of the mind to sustain its attention on the object of meditation without being distracted by extraneous sense objects. Concentration dispels the wandering tendencies of the mind while it unifies and integrates the mental factors.

Concentration is fostered by keeping the mental factors in balance. If the mind is lethargic, depressed, or lacks energy, we encourage the mind by focusing on the investigation of dhammas, energy, and rapture. If the mind is agitated or restless, we calm the mind by developing tranquillity, concentration, and equanimity. If doubt enters the mind or we feel discouragement concerning the practice or our ability to achieve results, we inspire the mind by reflecting on the qualities of the Buddha, Dhamma, and Sangha. Once the mind reaches a state of balance and concentration is present, we observe the mind with equanimity and avoid interfering with its functioning.

A further support to the development of concentration is to avoid individuals who are not bent on attaining concentration and to cultivate relationships with those who have already achieved it. Creating the intention or aspiration to remain concentrated while engaged in all activities also contributes to its maturation.

The final factor of enlightenment is *equanimity*. In this context, equanimity is not the neutral spiritual feeling discussed as part of the second foundation of mindfulness. It refers to an impartial perspective regarding consciousness and its associated mental factors. Equanimity observes the mental factors and, where there is a lack of balance, introduces the appropriate remedy to restore the effective functioning of the mind. Equanimity arises gradually as the six preceding factors of enlightenment come to maturity.

The development of equanimity is supported by cultivating a non-attached attitude toward all living beings and inanimate objects. Non-attachment is not the same as detachment (which has a subtle resistance associated with it) or indifference. Non-attachment is similar to a mirror that reflects whatever it sees without any grasping or resistance. It is a non-preferential quality of mind that does not react to that which it encounters. We develop this non-attachment and equanimous quality of mind as the investigation of dhammas shows us that all conditioned experience is ultimately impermanent, unsatisfactory, and selfless.

To cultivate equanimity, it is helpful to avoid individuals who are so attached to their relationships, pets, or possessions that they resist looking at the transitory nature of life. We need to develop associations with those who face this truth and are striving to cultivate a balanced mind. Finally, as with the other factors of enlightenment, maintaining a strong commitment to achieving equanimity supports its unfolding.

The Four Noble Truths

The Four Noble Truths are the final objects of contemplation in the *Mahasatipatthana Sutta*. According to the Buddha, the penetration of these truths is what constituted his own enlightenment. The First Truth states that life is inherently problematic and filled with suffering. The Second Truth explains how craving creates and perpetuates this suffering. The Third Noble Truth reveals that the way to end the suffering is to end the craving and to experience the freedom of the unconditioned reality. The Fourth Noble Truth describes the Noble Eightfold Path, which directly leads to the end of craving and hence to the end of suffering. There is a specific task to be fulfilled in association with each truth: suffering is to be fully understood; craving is to be fully abandoned; the unconditioned reality, nibbana, is to be fully realized; and the Noble Eightfold Path is to be fully developed.

In the First Noble Truth, the Buddha describes the scope of suffering that we experience. Suffering begins at birth with the trauma of being thrust into the world from the relative comfort and security of the womb. Birth marks the commencement of the suffering we will experience during the rest of our life.

Aging, too, is suffering. As we age, we experience the decay of the physical body; for example, the hair turns gray, the teeth break apart, the body wrinkles, the muscles sag, the senses dull, the limbs become weak, the organs begin to fail, and the energy level declines. Aging also weakens the mental faculties; for example, the memory begins to fade, it takes longer to recall information, and the mind becomes easily confused. When we age, society's attitude toward us changes. We may be cast aside by our families, placed in nursing homes without our consent, talked about as if we were not in the room, and treated as if we were children. We may also experience anxiety as we consider our impending death.

Death is suffering because we do not want to leave our loved ones, possessions, and memories. When death approaches, we may feel overwhelmed due to our unresolved issues. The process of dying may be accompanied by intense physical pain and mental anguish.

Suffering comes from sorrow, lamentation, pain, grief, and despair. Sorrow is the sadness that arises when we experience loss or disappointment. Lamentation is the point at which our sorrow becomes so great that we are brought to tears. We experience physical pain as a result of illness, accidents, unfavorable weather conditions, and so on. Grief, or mental pain, arises from unhappiness, fear, and anxiety. Despair, the most profound form of psychological suffering, occurs when we feel helpless to change our circumstances, and life seems hopeless.

Association with what we dislike, such as unpleasant or disagreeable sense objects, thoughts, feelings, individuals, and environmental conditions, is suffering. Separation from what brings us happiness, comfort, and feelings of security is suffering.

Not getting what we want is suffering. We want to stay young and healthy, to never die, and to reach all of our goals. However, we age, fall ill, die, and are unable to realize our aspirations. Even to reach our goals is suffering since that which we acquire is always impermanent.

As a summation of the First Noble Truth, the Buddha states that, "in short, the five aggregates of clinging is suffering." By this statement the Buddha is pointing out that everything within the scope of our experience is ultimately a source of suffering.

We view material forms, feelings, perceptions, mental formations, and consciousness as being our self, and desperately cling to these aggregates. Since they are impermanent, conditioned, follow their own laws, and are beyond our control, a subtle but deep sense of loss is continuously being experienced. These mini-deaths, which occur during every moment of our lives, are the most profound and pervasive source of our suffering.

The Buddha tells us that suffering needs to be fully understood. Many people would call this a pessimistic view of life and wonder why the Buddha did not focus on the joys of living. It is quite pleasant to eat delicious foods, to listen to good music, to raise a family, or to successfully reach our goals. However, since everything in the world is impermanent, even the greatest joy ultimately leads to an unsatisfactory experience. In order to acknowledge the pleasures that exist while still pointing to their limitations, some commentators use the word "unsatisfactoriness," as opposed to "suffering," to describe the First Noble Truth.

Examining our suffering is often the antithesis of what we try to do in our life. Therefore, in a sense, looking at our suffering tends to create more suffering. However, the purpose of facing the extent of our suffering is to motivate us to uncover its cause and to end this suffering once and for all. There are several contemplations that expose the scope of the unsatisfactory nature of experience. These are not intellectual exercises. We need to be careful to avoid making any judgments, decisions, or commentary based on what we experience and to allow the results of the exercises to speak for themselves.

For the first contemplation, mentally note each time you experience physical or mental suffering throughout the day. On the physical level, you may feel headaches, pains in your body, chest congestion, stomach cramps, and so forth. Psychologically, you may feel frustrated, sad, guilty, fearful, disappointed, worried, irritated, anxious, and so on. Practice this contemplation until you come to recognize just how pervasive the experience of physical and mental suffering actually is.

For the second contemplation, mentally note each time you are engaged in an activity for the express purpose of maintaining the body. For example, note each time you feed the body, provide the body with liquids, clean the body, answer the calls of nature, clothe the body, take medication, blow the nose, cough to remove congestion, and so forth. Continue with this exercise until you realize how bound up your life is with catering to the incessant demands of the body.

For the third contemplation, mentally note when a pleasant feeling arises. Observe the impermanence of that feeling, and focus very precisely on the sense of sorrow, disappointment, frustration, or loss that may arise as a consequence of having that pleasant experience disappear. The objective of this contemplation is to realize the more subtle forms of mental suffering, which we frequently experience.

During these contemplations, the thought may spontaneously

arise that "Just as I experience these forms of suffering, so does everyone else." From this meaningful realization, deep feelings of loving-kindness and compassion will begin to flow from our hearts.

Having opened our eyes to the scope of suffering that we experience, the Buddha now addresses the cause of that suffering. It is said that while other teachers are like dogs, the Buddha is like a lion. When you throw a stick at a dog, the dog chases the stick. When you throw a stick at a lion, however, the lion chases the person who threw the stick! Similarly, while other teachers speak about reducing the symptoms of suffering, the Buddha goes directly to the cause of suffering with the goal of ending our suffering once and for all.

In the Second Noble Truth, the Buddha explains that it is our craving, our unquenchable "thirst," or self-centered desire to have our experiences meet the demands of our ego, that lies at the root of our suffering. The more craving we have, the more suffering we experience.

We must remember, however, that there is no self that craves. There is no independent entity that reaches out through the sense doors and grasps at experiences in the hopes of either reducing suffering or of experiencing additional sensual pleasures. Craving arises due to a series of physical and psychological events that condition its appearance. Craving keeps recurring because the causes and conditions for its reappearance keep recurring. This looping chain of events, referred to as dependent origination, perpetuates the craving and the illusion of a self that craves and experiences the results of that craving.

As part of our description of the stages of purification, we have been exploring some of the links to this conditioned chain of events. The Second Noble Truth, however, clarifies the entire process. This dependently originated chain of events operates due to a lawful process that can be stated as:

> When this is, that comes to be;
> With the arising of this, that arises.
> When this is not, that does not come to be;
> With the cessation of this, that ceases.

These statements, spoken by the Buddha, refer to the fact that when the causes and conditions are put into place for the arising of any phenomenon, the arising of that phenomenon is certain to occur. These phrases also indicate that when those causes and conditions are no longer in place, the phenomenon will no longer be capable of arising.

The usual way in which the dependent origination process is explained is as it occurs over three lifetimes. By presenting it in this manner, we can understand how our present life is a result of the causes and conditions from our past life and how our next life will be influenced by the causes and conditions from our current life. However, the entire dependent origination process is in operation during each moment of our experience. This moment-to-moment playing out of the dependent origination process will be the focus of our discussion of the Second Noble Truth. The twelve links of dependent origination are summarized in table 5 (on page 116).

The series of events that occurs as part of the dependent origination process is not linear in nature, whereby a single cause is responsible for creating a single effect. Multiple causes are responsible for creating each effect. Each effect, in turn becomes one of many causes responsible for producing many other effects. Although there is no discoverable "first cause" to this chain of events, we will begin exploring the series of links with the factor of *ignorance*, which is a source of nourishment that feeds and sustains the entire process.

Ignorance can be defined as delusion or spiritual blindness. It manifests as clinging to a view of self when the impermanent, unsatisfactory, and selfless nature of experience has not been realized. This view of self is reinforced through each link in this conditioned chain of events.

In dependence upon ignorance (and other associated causes), there arise volitional formations. Volitional formations, also referred to as kamma, are the words, thoughts, and deeds intentionally committed by individuals who are still under the influence of ignorance. Whenever we perform an intentional action (which includes speech and thought), that action has the potential to create a series of results. The results will manifest in accord with the following universal principles.

Everything in the universe exists as a form of energy, and as such, is in a constant state of flux. Mental intention is a subtle form of this same energy. Although everything is subject to change, nothing is ever lost or destroyed in the process; only the forms of things change. For example, ice changes to water and water changes to vapor. In other words, everything is constantly becoming something other than it was just a moment before.

The entire universe is interconnected and interdependent. It is similar to a spider web: If you touch one part of the web, the entire web shimmers. We live in one integrated ecosystem. That which occurs in the rainforests, as we know, affects the entire planet.

The law of attraction states that forms of energy vibrating at the same frequency tend to be drawn to each other. In other words, like attracts like—birds of a feather really do flock together. Individuals generally form relationships with others who share the same moral values. We always attract those people and circumstances that are in accord with our deepest and most sincere intentions.

Finally, for every action there is a corresponding reaction. However, as we have discussed, this cause and effect is not linear, with a one-to-one correspondence between an action and its result. Even when we put the correct causes into place, we may not immediately see the results that we would expect. Other causes may be working to prevent or delay the manifestation of those results.

To apply these principles to the law of kamma, when an action is committed with an intention (a volitional formation) to produce a particular result, that intention flows out into the universe as a form of energy. This energy will not be lost or destroyed. Having no physical boundaries or limitations, the intention will interconnect with the rest of the universe and attract to itself those conditions that correspond to the very nature of the intention.

Some individuals report experiencing synchronicity or meaningful coincidences in their lives. Actually, every moment of our lives is synchronistic. Our lives are a reflection of our past intentions in conjunction with our present intentions.

If this is the case, we may wonder why we are not yet seeing the results of the wholesome intentions we have been struggling to generate. There are three reasons why this may be occurring in our lives. First, our intentions may not have had enough intensity or consistency to generate immediate results. Second, we may have unconsciously been creating intentions that run counter to the ones we are consciously trying to manifest. Finally, strong intentions, or kamma from our past, may be coming to fruition and inhibiting the manifestation of the results from our more recent intentions. We need to keep in mind that it is not our self that creates the intentions or experiences the results of our kamma. Intentions arise based upon our level of spiritual development and the ongoing conditioning of the mind. The results we experience come about through the natural playing out of the laws that govern kamma.

The next link in the chain is consciousness. In dependence upon the wholesome and unwholesome volitional formations of the past, sense consciousness arises in each present moment along with sensory experiences that correspond to the nature of the kamma previously committed. As we discussed, consciousness is actually a continuum of momentary states of consciousness. As each moment of consciousness disappears, it transmits to the next moment of consciousness all of its stored memories and impressions. This process takes place even though we may not be aware that it is occurring. As a result of the transmission of influence and memory, the illusion of a permanent and stable self is perpetuated.

In dependence upon consciousness, mental and physical phenomena arise. Consciousness is the supporting condition for the arising of materiality (the physical form) and mental formations (including feelings and perceptions). Without consciousness, the body would die and the mental formations would no longer arise. It is in relation to the five aggregates that the view of self is constructed.

In dependence upon mental and physical phenomena, the six (internal) sense bases arise. In other words, without the physical body and the mind as a supporting condition, the six sense organs could not operate. It is through one or another of these sense organs that each sensory experience occurs. The sense organs function as the basis for the arising of sense consciousness (eye consciousness, ear consciousness, and so forth).

In dependence upon the six sense bases, contact arises. Opposed to physical contact, this contact is said to occur when the mind experiences a sense object. Whenever a sense object, sense organ, and corresponding sense consciousness come together, sense contact is said to occur.

In dependence upon contact, feeling arises. Whenever a sense object is contacted through any of the six sense doors, a pleasant, unpleasant, or neutral feeling will occur. The particular quality of the feeling we experience within the context of the process of dependent origination will be a result of our past kamma.

Feeling is a critical link in this dependently originated chain of events. We made reference to its significance when we discussed "guarding the sense doors" and again when we reviewed mindfulness of feelings. As long as we are alive, our mind will make contact with sense objects through our six sense organs. Each time that occurs, a feeling will choicelessly arise. If we do not place a wedge of mindful awareness between the feeling and craving (the next link in the chain), we have lost a pivotal opportunity to break the sequence of events that keeps us in spiritual bondage. This wedge of awareness enables us to recognize the impermanent, unsatisfactory, and selfless nature of each feeling, preventing the mind from creating unwholesome kamma by reacting to that feeling with greed, hatred, or delusion.

In dependence upon feeling, craving arises. Craving is referred to as the Second Noble Truth, or the source of our suffering. It is considered such because, by missing the opportunity to break the dependently originated chain of events at the point of feeling, our craving forms the basis of unwholesome kamma, which continues to create causes and conditions for suffering to arise in the future.

The three types of craving are sense craving, craving for existence, and craving for non-existence. Sense craving is the desire for pleasant sensory experiences, which arise when contact is made through any of the six sense doors.

Craving for existence is the wish to go on living. It is the most powerful force in the universe. It can manifest as the desire for an eternal afterlife, as the fear of death, or more subtly as the wish to make a contribution that will live on after we are gone.

Craving for non-existence, or annihilation, is the desire to end one's life. When issues appear to be unsolvable, an individual may desire to end his or her existence. A subtle form of this craving for annihilation occurs for meditators when they see the self as the enemy and want to destroy it. We cannot kill or destroy something, however, that never existed.

In dependence upon craving, clinging arises. Clinging is an intensified form of craving. The nature of clinging is to tightly grasp that which the mind craves. We cling to sensual pleasures, wrong views regarding the nature of the world, the idea that rites and rituals can purify the mind, and the belief in the existence of a self.

In dependence upon clinging, existence arises. This link in the dependent origination chain refers to the existence of kamma—generated as a result of clinging—and to the existence of the results of that kamma. The difference between existence and volitional formations is that volitional formations only point to the intentional aspect of kamma. Here, existence refers to the fact that the intentional and resultant aspects of kamma are constantly alternating within consciousness in each moment of our lives.

In dependence upon existence, birth arises. When we identify with our feelings and allow craving, clinging, and kamma to manifest, the birth of our self-concept occurs. The emerging of this mentally constructed self is sustained throughout the dependent origination process as a result of ignorance, or not seeing things as they really are.

In dependence upon birth, aging and death arise. With the concept of birth (of a self) comes the concept of death (of a self). As a consequence of maintaining the view of having a self that is born and dies, there is an ongoing experience of sorrow, lamentation, pain, grief, and despair—what the Buddha referred to as the whole mass of suffering.

TABLE 5
THE TWELVE LINKS OF DEPENDENT ORIGINATION

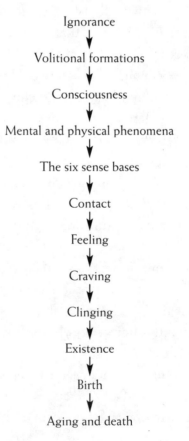

Ignorance
↓
Volitional formations
↓
Consciousness
↓
Mental and physical phenomena
↓
The six sense bases
↓
Contact
↓
Feeling
↓
Craving
↓
Clinging
↓
Existence
↓
Birth
↓
Aging and death

As a result of investigating the dependently arisen chain of events that keeps us tied to the sensual world, with its attendant suffering, the question as to whether there is "free will" may arise. Will is merely another mental factor that rises and falls based upon specific causes and conditions. There is no permanent state of will that is or is not free. Nonetheless, we are still responsible for our moment-to-moment choices. We need to be sure that we are intentionally choosing skillful or wholesome courses of action.

Once the mind recognizes the nature of craving and how it perpetuates suffering, the desire to abandon that craving will naturally arise. The following exercises support the understanding of how craving operates in our lives.

The first contemplation is simple but quite powerful. We want to become completely clear that sense craving is insatiable. Try to discover anything in your life for which each of the following three conditions are totally true. First, that there is something in your life with which you are completely satisfied (it could be a relationship, possession, circumstance, and so on). Second, that you have no desire whatsoever to change or modify that with which you are satisfied. Finally, that you have absolutely no resistance to losing that fulfilling aspect of your life.

For the next contemplation, reflect on how the craving for existence has expressed itself in your life. Consider, for example, how the fear of dying may have arisen when an airplane in which you were flying suddenly hit an air pocket. Think about concerns that arose the last time you were seriously ill. Reflect on any desire you may have to make a difference and to leave your "mark" in the world. Finally, consider any wish you may have to be reborn in heaven, or some subsequent life, after you die.

For the third contemplation, observe the suffering that is inherent to all craving. The moment that craving arises, recognize how the mind began craving without any conscious control on your part. Next, look for the subtle sense of insufficiency that actually motivated the craving. Finally, notice that the amount of suffering being experienced is in direct proportion to the strength of the craving that is present.

With the abandoning of craving there is the cessation of suffering, which corresponds to the attainment of the Third Noble Truth. When the conditioned, dependently originated chain of events that has kept us in spiritual bondage is broken, we realize nibbana, the unconditioned reality. *Nibbana* literally means "to extinguish," and what is extinguished are the fires of lust, hatred, and delusion.

Nibbana cannot be adequately described since it is a reality that transcends all conceptual categories. The mind can only think within a limited dualistic framework, from which it views experience in terms of alternatives: love or hate, joy or sorrow, freedom or bondage, and so forth. It is not possible for the mind to recognize the nondualistic actuality that lies beyond its own experience. As a result, the Buddha often described nibbana using negative qualifiers, such as the "the unconditioned," "the unborn," and "the undying." However, the actual experience of nibbana is beyond both positive and negative mental constructs.

The greatest paradox is that the spiritual freedom for which we are searching is already ours. It is similar to the sun, which while being obscured by clouds, remains ever present behind them. Nibbana, the transcendent experience of liberation, is forever present beyond the clouds of our own delusion. We will explore this unconditioned reality in greater depth when we discuss the seventh stage of purification.

Without experiencing the seventh stage of purification, there are no contemplations that will give us an immediate and firsthand experience of nibbana. We can, however, experience the freedom that arises when the mind temporarily lets go of craving. For this exercise, each time you realize that you are experiencing some form of psychological suffering, mindfully observe the craving that is present at that moment. As previously discussed, when we apply mindfulness in this manner, the unwholesome state of mind we are observing is actually no longer present. It is the wake or impression left in the mind from the craving and suffering of which we are currently aware.

Now, immediately turn your attention to the experience of mindfulness. In other words, become mindful of the moment of mindfulness that just occurred. Experience the release from craving and suffering that arose when mindfulness was present. Allow your mind to become intimate with this wonderful taste of freedom.

The Fourth Noble Truth describes the path that leads directly to the relinquishment of craving, to the cessation of suffering, and to the realization of nibbana—the unconditioned reality. This remarkable teaching is referred to as the Noble Eightfold Path. The factors of this path are divided into three sections: the morality section, which consists of right speech, right action, and right livelihood; the concentration section, which includes right effort, right mindfulness, and right concentration; and the wisdom section, which encompasses right view and right intention.

The explanation of the path usually begins and ends with the two factors from the wisdom group: right view and right intention. The purpose is to demonstrate that we begin our spiritual development with a conceptual understanding of what is meant by the Four Noble Truths, and we finish our inward journey with a direct realization of what these truths represent. We will discuss each path factor in turn.

Right view, at this point, is a theoretical understanding of the Four Noble Truths, the framework within which all of the Buddha's teachings are contained. The Four Noble Truths elucidate the scope of suffering that we experience, the ways in which kamma operates to perpetuate or eliminate that suffering, and how the systematic cultivation of virtue, concentration, and wisdom leads to spiritual liberation. It is essential to develop right view since our views govern all of our decisions, actions, and ultimately the spiritual results we achieve.

Right intention refers to the volitional aspect of thought, as opposed to the mind's cognitive function. The volitional property of thought determines whether our words, thoughts, and deeds are kammically wholesome or unwholesome. There are three types of right thought: thoughts of renunciation, thoughts of loving-kindness, and thoughts of compassion.

Renunciation is the intention to simplify and streamline our life to make it more conducive to the work of mental cultivation. The key to spiritual growth is to renounce sense craving, craving for existence, and craving for non-existence, each of which perpetuates our experience of suffering. Renunciation also refers to abandoning the attachment to our limited and distorted views and allowing the truth of each experience to speak for itself.

Loving-kindness is the intention to have all living beings be well, happy, and peaceful. The most significant barrier to the expression of loving-kindness is harboring anger and resentment toward ourselves or toward those who have treated us badly in the past. Our anger cannot change what has already transpired. Hateful intentions lead to unskillful behaviors and destroy our potential to experience the benefits of living with an open heart, free from all enmity.

Compassion is the intention to relieve the suffering of others. It arises with the recognition of the universality of suffering and the realization that all living beings desire happiness. We need to express compassion through our actions and not just hold it as a thought in our mind.

Right speech, the first factor in the morality section, has four aspects to it: abstaining from false speech, abstaining from slanderous speech, abstaining from harsh speech, and abstaining from idle chatter. Speech is very powerful. Since there is always an intention motivating our speech, our speech has significant kammic consequences. Speech is capable of creating both concord and discord. It can be used to manipulate or to teach others the deep meaning of the Dhamma.

Although the four facets of right speech are expressed in negative terms ("abstaining from"), each facet has a positive counterpart. Abstaining from false speech, for example, means to always speak the truth, while remaining sensitive to the potential impact of our communication. As discussed under the purification of virtue, we should avoid even what appear to be harmless lies. At times, maintaining "noble silence" is the best response to an awkward or difficult situation. The Buddha taught that we should not tell a lie, even when relating the truth puts our life at risk. Telling the truth is also essential for realizing "Ultimate Truth," since to do so our mind must be aligned with truth at every level.

Slanderous speech is using words that intentionally create dissension between individuals. Slander, or the carrying of stories from one person to another, is sometimes used to place oneself in a position of power or as a way to gain approval from others. We should always speak words that encourage individuals to develop friendships and to be grateful for the friendships that they already have. Speech that strives to bring harmony easily flows from a mind filled with loving-kindness and compassion.

When speech is painful to hear because of cruel or offensive language, or because it is spoken to us with a stern tone of voice, the speech is considered harsh. We may speak harshly when we are angry or lose our patience. In a striking example, the Buddha tells his disciples that "even if bandits were to savagely sever your limbs with a two-handled saw, your minds should remain unaffected, and you should still not utter any harsh words." The Buddha says that all words spoken should be "gentle, soothing to the ear, loving, such words as go to the heart and are courteous, friendly, and agreeable to many."

Abstaining from idle chatter involves not wasting time speaking of things that lead only to the perpetuation of delusion. The Buddha mentioned several topics ideally to be avoided, including talking about politics, armies, war, crime, cities, modes of transportation, clothing, food, drink, sexuality, and relatives. In addition, the Buddha advised his listeners to eliminate all forms of gossip. The only thing left to speak about, then, is the Dhamma—and thus our speech is conducive to our spiritual growth and the attainment of liberation.

We already addressed the next two path factors, right action and right livelihood, when we discussed the purification of virtue. Right action includes: abstaining from killing and acting with reverence toward all forms of life; abstaining from stealing and cultivating generosity; and abstaining from sexual misconduct, while remaining sensitive to the needs of all those with whom we are intimate. Right livelihood involves abstaining from forms of livelihood that bring harm

to other beings, while engaging in work that supports the fulfillment of our financial, social, creative, psychological, and
spiritual needs.

Right effort, the next factor of the Noble Eightfold Path, is
the first of three factors concerned with developing concentration (the other two are right mindfulness and right concentration). There are four types of right effort: the effort to
prevent unskillful mental states from arising, the effort to eliminate unskillful mental states that have already arisen, the effort
to cultivate skillful mental states, and the effort to sustain skillful mental states that have already arisen.

The most effective way to prevent the arising of unskillful
mental states is to "stand guard at our sense doors," with mindfulness acting as the sentry. We addressed this technique when
we discussed the purification of virtue. At that time we indicated that an important place to stand guard was between the
feeling, which arises in dependence upon sense contact, and
any craving that may arise based upon that feeling. By watching the rising and falling of each feeling, we are able to short-
circuit unskillful states before they take root in our mind.

It is also possible to stand guard at the sense doors at an
earlier stage, at the point of pure sense contact. The goal is to
prevent any conceptual proliferation from arising, which usually occurs when the mind is allowed to dwell on the sense data
that comes through the six sense doors. We are to stop at the
point of bare sense contact and merely see forms, hear sounds,
smell odors, taste flavors, touch tangible objects, think
thoughts, and so forth. This is the pure experience of consciousness rising and falling along with its object. By guarding
the sense doors in this manner, there is no room for the mind
to form concepts of self or other concepts that may become the
basis for the arising of greed, hatred, or delusion.

The Buddha gives a succinct set of instructions on how to practice this contemplation to a recluse named Bahiya:

> Then, Bahiya, thus must you train yourself: "In the seen, there will be just the seen; in the heard, just the heard; in the sensed, just the sensed; in the cognized, just the cognized." That is how, Bahiya, you must train yourself.

The Buddha suggests several ways to eliminate unskillful states once they have arisen. One technique is to replace an unwholesome thought with its direct opposite. If a thought rooted in greed arises, for example, we would replace it with one based upon generosity. If a thought rooted in hatred arises, we would replace it with a thought based on loving-kindness.

A second method is to consider the undesirable consequences of allowing unskillful states to remain in the mind. The result of worry, for example, is the experience of anxiety, stress, and fear. The result of anger could be a loss of control, distorted thinking, diminished self-respect, and a closed heart. These considerations may provide the impetus for us to remove unskillful states.

A third process is to investigate the source of the unskillful states that have arisen. If we feel angry, for example, we can examine the mind to determine the origin of that anger. When we discover that the anger originated from our reactions to unpleasant feelings, which arose based upon our negative perceptions of what we were experiencing and not from the experience itself, the anger may dissipate on its own.

The effort to cultivate wholesome states entails introducing the factors that are part of the Noble Eightfold Path or those included in the four foundations of mindfulness. Once any of these factors has arisen, we want them to remain in our mind as long as possible and to utilize them to support mental purification and the realization of spiritual liberation.

The final two path factors, right mindfulness and right concentration, are the last two factors of the concentration section. Right mindfulness is the ongoing contemplation of the four foundations of mindfulness: the body, feelings, consciousness, and dhammas. Right concentration is synonymous with purification of mind, the second stage of purification.

After each factor of the Noble Eightfold Path has been thoroughly understood and practiced, we come back to right view and right intention. At this point, however, the experience of these factors is the result of wisdom, rather than an intellectual understanding. By developing the Noble Eightfold Path in this manner, we have fulfilled Buddha's requirement for the Fourth Noble Truth.

KNOWLEDGE BY COMPREHENSION

The truth concerning the impermanent, unsatisfactory, and selfless nature of all conditioned phenomena will deeply impress itself upon our mind as the contemplations related to mindfulness of consciousness and mindfulness of dhammas are practiced. Impermanence will be fully comprehended after repeatedly seeing for ourselves that each object that arises to consciousness, along with consciousness itself, immediately undergoes destruction or dissolution. The unsatisfactory nature of the five aggregates will be comprehended after recognizing that it is not possible for any of the aggregates to offer a lasting sense of peace, security, or satisfaction. Selflessness will be comprehended after realizing that every dhamma that is experienced is without a substantial core, or an inherent self that endures through time.

At this stage of development, through inductive reasoning, it will occur to us that all conditioned phenomena arising in the past were also governed by impermanence, unsatisfactoriness, and selflessness. Further, we will perceive that all conditioned phenomena that will arise in the future will also be subject to these same three properties. We will, in fact, realize that every conditioned phenomena connected with the five aggregates is nothing more than an expression of these three characteristics.

The scope of understanding regarding the presence of these characteristics is different for each meditator. For some, the understanding of the true nature of the aggregates will easily be applied to external sets of aggregates (those of other individuals). For others, the understanding will extend to all phenomena, whether animate or inanimate. However, when the direct and spontaneous comprehension of the true nature of our own aggregates is clearly seen, one has attained knowledge by comprehension.

THE INITIAL PHASE OF THE
KNOWLEDGE OF ARISING AND PASSING AWAY

As a result of practicing the contemplations associated with consciousness and the dhammas, we have a more thorough recognition of the conditioned and dependently arisen nature of the five aggregates. We have seen that formations arise when the conditions for their arising are in place and that formations cease when those conditions are no longer present. This deeper understanding of the causes and conditions responsible for the perpetuation of the aggregates indicates the presence of the initial phase of the knowledge of arising and passing away. Certain profound experiences begin to arise at this point. If we become attached to these experiences, or believe that their presence indicates that we have attained enlightenment, the experiences are termed "imperfections" or "corruptions" of insight.

THE TEN CORRUPTIONS OF INSIGHT

There are ten corruptions of insight: illumination, knowledge, rapture, calm, bliss, faith, energy, mindfulness, equanimity, and attachment. These corruptions arise in no particular order, and not every meditator will encounter or even notice the presence of each one.

The perception of an illumination or of a bright light may be seen with our eyes opened or closed. It may appear similar to a locomotive headlight or to the light that emanates from a powerful lamp. We may even perceive this light as issuing from our own body. We may become fascinated with the light and not want to watch it rise and fall as simply another object of awareness.

Knowledge, or the understanding of aspects of the Dhamma that we did not fully understand in the past, may now become clear to us. The meaning of specific terms, the understanding of how aspects of the path integrate, the comprehension of dependent origination, and other difficult concepts, may now be easily understood. We may feel that our mind is in accord with our teacher's mind, and the desire to begin teaching may arise. We may even believe that our level of attainment has surpassed that of our teacher, and disagreements with him or her may ensue.

The experience of rapture or joy may be overwhelming. Any of the five grades of rapture (minor, momentary, showering, uplifting, or pervading), described earlier as aspects of the first jhanic experience, may become prominent. It may be difficult for us to just watch the experience of rapture rise and fall. We may even believe that we have reached the end of the path and consequently stop practicing.

Although the experience of a deep and penetrating calm may have arisen at various times throughout our practice, the feelings of bodily and mental peace that occur at this stage are more pervasive and profound. The body is cool and comfortable, and the mind is relaxed. Each movement of the body and mind is effortless, and the process of noticing the rise and fall of all phenomena proceeds smoothly. We may become content with this significant experience of tranquillity and not desire to forgo it for the sake of cultivating additional insight.

A profound sense of bliss or happiness may arise. At this stage the experience of happiness feels all-encompassing, since it is present even during times when we are not engaged in formal meditation. We may believe that this is the happiness for which we have been searching, and we may want to communicate to everyone what we are feeling. A deep sense of gratitude for the teacher may arise. The experience of intense and overwhelming rapture, calm, or bliss is the result of an imbalance between effort and concentration, with too much focus on concentration.

We may experience exceptional faith in the Buddha, Dhamma, and Sangha. This strong sense of faith, devotion, or inspiration may even bring us to tears. Gratitude and a strong desire to support the teacher or the meditation center may surface. Great enthusiasm for continuing the practice may arise; we may even have thoughts of ordaining or remaining at the meditation center until the final stages of purification are achieved. Faith will need to be balanced by discernment or discrimination for the further stages of insight to occur.

A powerful energy may arise, and with it an absence of any sleepiness or lethargic feelings. We may be able to meditate for extended periods of time without difficulty, noticing the object of our meditation with balanced effort. We may believe that this energy is a permanent condition and fail to recognize its conditioned and impermanent nature.

Mindfulness may arise without any apparent effort on our part. It is almost as if mindfulness reaches toward the objects that arise to consciousness under its own power. We may believe that there is no condition of mind that will arise of which we will not be mindful. We may be deceived, thinking that enlightenment has been reached, since we have perfect mindfulness. However, for further insight knowledges to come to fruition, mindfulness itself needs to be seen with mindfulness.

With the arising of equanimity comes an ease in discerning the three characteristics of experience. This is not the equanimity previously described as a neutral spiritual feeling. In this context, equanimity is the ability of the mind to penetrate every formation that arises without effort. The true nature of each formation immediately becomes apparent. We may, at this point, believe that all defilements have been eradicated and decide to stop practicing. In actuality, the defilements have only been suppressed. Wrong view remains until the very last stage of purification is reached.

The final corruption of insight is attachment, which may arise as a result of the delight we derive from the profound occurrences we experience. We may not recognize the very subtle attachments we have developed, and may believe that the experiences result from a supramundane attainment. This becomes a barrier to further practice and spiritual development. It is the presence of this attachment that is the deciding factor as to whether these experiences are to be considered corruptions of insight.

Although there are meditators who can undergo these experiences and not mistakenly believe that they herald the attainment of enlightenment, it is rare for a meditator not to form a subtle attachment to one or all of them. Through the earnest application of mindfulness, or through the interaction with a skilled teacher, it becomes apparent that attachment to these experiences is not the path. When we can look upon these experiences as merely phenomena that rise and fall based upon causes and conditions, when we see that they exhibit the same three characteristics of all experience, we have finally reached the stage of the purification by knowledge and vision of what is the path and what is not the path.

THE WAY

Purification by knowledge and vision of the way is the last stage of spiritual development, prior to the direct realization of nibbana—the unconditioned reality. It is rich with insights and profound spiritual experiences. The prior stages of purification enabled us to intermittently recognize the specific attributes and universal characteristics of each experience. The knowledges associated with this stage of purification work toward eliminating the erroneous views that obscure our ability to see things as they really are on a more consistent basis.

Although there are nine insight knowledges associated with this stage of purification, more than twice as many as any other stage, we can experience all nine of them within moments of each other. It is an auspicious time when environmental, psychological, and spiritual causes and conditions coalesce in such a way that these profound knowledges begin to arise. We need to recognize this precious opportunity, maintain vigilance, and increase our effort in order to take full advantage of this rare set of circumstances.

Some of the insights that arise during this stage can be quite frightening, and it may feel as though we are actually losing our grip on reality rather than gaining a more secure one. Many of the insights may dramatically shift our point of view and cause confusion about the way to integrate our new perspective with our day-to-day lives. Without the guidance of a teacher or a thorough familiarity with what is actually occurring, some of the insights may cause us to temporarily back away from practice instead of pursuing it with more diligence.

Our discussion will begin with a description of an insight meditation practice that supports the arising of the knowledges that comprise this stage of purification.

REMAINING PRESENT WITH CHOICELESS AWARENESS

From the beginning of our practice of insight meditation, we have been using the breath (or another object from one of the four foundations of mindfulness) as the primary focus of our awareness. Whenever the mind strayed from this primary object, we noticed the impermanent, unsatisfactory, and selfless nature of the new object, and then gently but firmly returned to our breath. We used the primary object as an anchor that kept our awareness centered on what was occurring during each present moment. At this stage in our spiritual development, however, this practice technique has a significant drawback.

The purpose of insight meditation is to see things as they really are. In order for this to happen, we need to be choicelessly aware of whatever arises, without grasping or resisting any of our experiences. Whenever we have an intention to move our awareness in a particular direction (back to the breath, for example), we are subtly manipulating the mind by creating an intention, and we are no longer choicelessly aware of what is occurring.

Many meditators have learned to mentally note or label what they are experiencing as an aid to recognizing whatever is arising to consciousness. Although the noting may be heard as a very gentle voice in the mind, at this stage of practice the intention to note also becomes an impediment. It prevents us from being choicelessly aware of whatever is unfolding in each present moment. However, if the mind notes what it sees without any conscious intention on our part, noting is just treated as another object to watch rise and fall.

At this point in our practice, we no longer attend to any primary object. We just remain choicelessly aware of whatever arises to consciousness. Our prior work with the four foundations of mindfulness will now bear its greatest fruit. By intentionally having investigated the various aspects of the five aggregates, our mind will be less inclined to find interest in any of the phenomena it experiences. Since we are not grasping or resisting our sensory experiences, they will appear to arise and dissolve with remarkable speed. This recognition will enable us to gain deeper insights into the impermanent, unsatisfactory, and selfless nature of all conditioned phenomena.

In order for us to meditate in this manner, our momentary concentration needs to be well developed. It requires that we stay present with the waves of sensory experience as they incessantly break on the shore of our consciousness. If during this practice our mind loses its balance and gets swept away with what is being experienced, we return to using the breath as an anchor until our momentary concentration has regained its stability. Once that occurs, we let go of the breath, once again remaining choicelessly present with whatever is occurring.

THE MATURE PHASE OF THE KNOWLEDGE
OF ARISING AND PASSING AWAY

The current stage of purification begins to unfold as the insight knowledge of arising and passing away comes to maturity. This occurs after we have worked through the corruptions of insight, and our observation of the conditioned and dependently arisen nature of the aggregates continues unimpeded by perceptual distortions.

Normally, the characteristic of impermanence is concealed by the illusion of continuity. With our increased capacity to remain mindful, we come to realize that each and every object rises and falls, changes from moment to moment, and at no time exists as anything other than a process of becoming. Each object is seen to rise and fall in stages. Mindfulness becomes precise, and the impermanent nature of all phenomena is observed with great clarity.

The characteristic of pain, or the unsatisfactory nature of experience, is concealed by the change of postures and the perpetual movement of the mind. Bodily pain is especially hard to bear since the desire for sensual pleasure is so great. When we focus our attention on the body while maintaining our commitment not to move, however, we directly experience that the body is perpetually on fire with discomfort. As we continue to remain choicelessly aware of what is occurring within the mind, we are able to recognize the intense desire to suppress or avoid all painful feelings. We begin to clearly discern the aggregates as being unsatisfactory due to their impermanent nature.

The characteristic of selflessness is concealed by the concept of compactness. What was previously believed to be a substantial entity is now seen as a dependently arisen succession of momentary occurrences of mind and matter. In the past, we had superimposed a mental construct of a self over these self-less processes. At this stage of practice, we penetrate this form of illusion and clearly recognize the vibratory and selfless nature of the body and mind.

The mature phase of the knowledge of arising and passing away represents an important stage in our practice. It is the base from which we can reach the remaining insight knowledges leading to spiritual liberation.

THE KNOWLEDGE OF DISSOLUTION

When the knowledge of arising and passing away comes to maturity, the incessant ceasing of each bodily and mental process will be clear to us. When this occurs, it is referred to as the knowledge of dissolution.

Phenomena now pass through the mind with the speed of a whirlwind. Each experience is seen to be dissolving moment by moment. As a consequence, the concept of a person or being also begins to dissolve. All that we have considered ourselves to be appears to be dying each moment.

We realize with crystal clarity that both consciousness and the object of consciousness disappear simultaneously. After each object of consciousness disappears, we are able to take as the next object of consciousness the thought that reflected upon the dissolution of the prior object of consciousness. The insight may arise that if a sense object is not presently the object of our consciousness, it cannot be said to exist. At some point, it may appear that mindfulness has been lost since the mind is only seeing phenomena disappearing, but this is certainly not the case.

THE KNOWLEDGE OF THE FEARFUL

When everything we notice is immediately seen to dissolve, our sense of security begins to disappear as well. An overwhelming fear or a great sense of terror may arise at this point. This experience is referred to as the knowledge of the fearful.

A thought may occur that "If this continues, I will completely disappear," or we may experience this knowledge as a generalized feeling of anxiety. On one retreat, an individual who experienced this intense fear grabbed a lamp and started shouting into it, "I am still here. I have not disappeared." One meditator described her experience of seeing everything dissolve as: "I am scared here. I am seeing things I have never seen before." Another individual related that, "At the point of going still deeper, fear suddenly came up and pulled me back from that experience."

Without the guidance of a teacher or a deep understanding of this phase of practice, we may think about stopping our meditation. At this point, however, we must remain present and "sit through the fear" with courageous energy. The fear is nothing more than another mental construct associated with feelings and bodily sensations. Some meditators approach this type of fear several times before they are able to stay present with the experience. Eventually, if we continue to make the effort to remain fully mindful of the fear, it will dissolve in the same way as everything else we have been noticing.

As the fear begins to diminish, it may be replaced by a deep sense of grief. The grief arises as a consequence of having seen the selfless nature of all that we have considered our self to be. When this occurs, we must remain courageously present with the grief, as we did with the fear.

THE KNOWLEDGE OF CONTEMPLATION OF DANGER

As we come to recognize that fear, grief, and all forms of suffering arise as a result of our clinging to the five aggregates, the danger in doing so becomes apparent. This understanding is the knowledge of contemplation of danger.

Whereas we previously feared losing our sense of self and of helplessly falling into some void, we now fear falling into the trap of once again identifying with any of the five aggregates. Wherever we turn, there appears to be no escape from this danger. Even the thought of being born in a heavenly realm of existence begins to lose its appeal. To pass through this stage, we must maintain the momentum of our practice and continue meditating until we reach the further insights that are part of this stage of purification.

THE KNOWLEDGE OF DISENCHANTMENT

As a consequence of seeing the danger in grasping at any of the aggregates, we naturally become disenchanted with all material or mental formations. This is called the knowledge of disenchantment. This disenchantment arises from wisdom and is accompanied by equanimity, as opposed to aversion.

The experience of disenchantment may extend to all areas of our life and we may discover that we cannot find comfort anywhere. At this point in our practice we may feel quite alone in the world. When the sense of disenchantment becomes intense, we may once again consider giving up our practice, believing that our meditation has led us to a dead end.

One meditator describes her experience as follows:

...being scared to look at what's been coming up, been coming for weeks now. I bravely sat tonight and looked at this "dread" straight in the face, and it's the face of death. Futility, endings, death—over and over again. The mind is too aware of the constant endings to find comfort in anything. I've been reverting to old ways of seeking pleasure, wanting something, anything, to make this feeling of futility go away. It's not working. Reverting does nothing but pour salt on the wound. The mind is feeling a lot of pain, sometimes feelings of hopelessness at ever finding relief. It occurred to me to give up meditating altogether.

Another meditator reports:

Try as I might, I have had difficulties with "special" feelings toward people. It is not that I don't care as much about them, it is just harder to feel the emotional love I used to feel. Emotions in general have suddenly lost a lot of their energy. I am quite happy, but I find it very hard to really feel emotional about anything right now.

At this stage we must not lose hope and stop our meditation. This is a crucial stage of practice, which must be worked through. Along with everything else we are experiencing, this stage is also impermanent.

THE DESIRE FOR DELIVERANCE

The positive side of the mind becoming disenchanted and wanting to sever its ties with the mundane is the desire for deliverance by experiencing the spiritual freedom that comes from the supramundane. The *Visuddhimagga* gives the following analogy, which illustrates the meditator's intense desire to escape the bonds of spiritual ignorance:

> Just as a fish caught in a net, a frog in a snake's jaws, a jungle fowl shut into a cage, a deer fallen into the clutches of a strong snare, a snake in the hands of a snake charmer, an elephant stuck fast in a great bog...just as these are desirous of being delivered, of finding an escape from these things, so too this meditator's mind is desirous of being delivered from the whole field of formations and escaping from it.

Difficulties encountered at this point may include becoming very restless and experiencing intense mental and physical discomfort. We may also mistake our desire to escape the mundane for wanting more comfort in a general sense. At this time, we may think about moving to another meditation center where we would feel more comfortable. The wish to end practice may arise once again. It requires an earnest commitment, and working with a skillful teacher at times, to enable us to move through this advanced and key stage of practice.

It is important to note that we may not be able to distinguish which particular insight knowledge we are actually experiencing, and that making such a distinction is not a requisite part of our practice. The insight knowledges of dissolution, of the fearful, of danger, of disenchantment, and of desire for deliverance are all related. Each knowledge leads directly to the next, and it is possible that we work through the entire sequence of these latter knowledges in one meditation session. When the knowledge of dissolution arises, therefore, we should let nothing dissuade us from continuing to meditate.

THE KNOWLEDGE OF RE-OBSERVATION

As a result of experiencing the insight knowledges that are part of this stage of purification, and because of our deep desire for spiritual deliverance, we recommit to the practice of observing the impermanent, unsatisfactory, and selfless nature of each sensory experience that arises. This recommitment to our basic insight meditation practice is referred to as "re-observation." Becoming aware that this is what we must do is the knowledge of re-observation.

Insight is now very keen, and mindfulness easily alights on the objects being noticed. Intense pain or discomfort may arise at this point, but we are able to remain present with each unpleasant experience until it dissolves. We may discover that some of our chronic physical difficulties are disappearing for good. We clearly recognize that we are making progress, and our commitment to achieving final liberation is very strong.

THE KNOWLEDGE OF EQUANIMITY TOWARD FORMATIONS

At this point, a clear, deep, and penetrating insight into the selfless nature of all phenomena arises. We recognize that all the aggregates are void of self. We realize, for example, that when visual consciousness takes the body as an object, only visual form and the consciousness of that visual form exists. At that moment, the touch of the body, the sound of the body, and even the concept of "body" does not exist. We know that it is merely light, color, and form arising and passing away along with the consciousness of those qualities.

We have been superimposing our view of a substantial self over the rising and falling of impermanent and empty phenomena. We now realize that no man, woman, husband, wife, dog, building, or self actually exists. What we had previously considered to be substantial forms of existence were merely reflections of our own conceptual overlays.

When the understanding of the selfless nature of all phenomena becomes clear to us, the grasping and resisting of formations that arise to consciousness ceases. The mind becomes equanimous and we notice the characteristics of experience effortlessly. The formations are seen to dissolve even before they fully take root in the mind.

Even if a painful feeling arises in the body, it will no longer disturb us. The experience of fear, ill will, joy, happiness, and so forth will no longer disturb the mind's impartial stance toward all formations. The mind strongly desires to reach the unconditioned. It is no longer concerned with mundane dramas and the illusory appearance of things. This is the knowledge of equanimity toward formations.

THE KNOWLEDGE OF CONFORMITY WITH TRUTH

In a relay race, the person to receive the baton begins running even before the present runner reaches his or her position on the track. In effect, the subsequent racer tries to conform to the pace of the current runner, so that the transition will be smooth. Similarly, the knowledge of conformity with truth assists the mind in making a smooth transition from taking the five aggregates as its objects of awareness, to taking unconditioned reality as its object. It does so by helping the mind conform to the thirty-seven factors of enlightenment (see table 6, on the following pages), which will arise when the supramundane realizations occur.

The knowledge of conformity with truth arises spontaneously as the knowledge of equanimity about formations comes to maturity. This is the last insight knowledge to arise before the supramundane realizations, and as is the case with some of the other knowledges, this insight knowledge may not be recognized by us as a separate stage of spiritual development.

TABLE 6

THE THIRTY-SEVEN FACTORS OF ENLIGHTENMENT

The four foundations of mindfulness
    Mindfulness of the body
    Mindfulness of feelings
    Mindfulness of consciousness
    Mindfulness of mental objects (dhammas)

The four right efforts
    The effort to prevent unskillful mental states from arising
    The effort to eliminate unskillful mental states that have
        already arisen
    The effort to cultivate skillful mental states
    The effort to sustain skillful mental states that have already arisen

The four means to the accomplishment of the Buddha's teaching
    Wholesome desire
    Energy
    Consciousness
    Investigation

The five spiritual faculties that need to be in balance
    Faith or confidence
    Energy
    Mindfulness
    Concentration
    Wisdom

The five powers unshakable by their opposites
    Faith or confidence
    Energy
    Mindfulness

Concentration
Wisdom

The seven factors of enlightenment
(from the *Mahasatipatthana Sutta*)
Mindfulness
Investigation of dhammas
Energy or effort
Rapture or joy
Tranquillity
Concentration
Equanimity

The eight path factors
Right view
Right intention
Right speech
Right action
Right livelihood
Right effort
Right mindfulness
Right concentration

PURIFICATION BY KNOWLEDGE AND VISION

Purification by knowledge and vision is the final stage of the purification process. It is our unwavering dedication to impeccable virtue, deep concentration, and the consistent practice of insight meditation that has brought us to this significant point in our spiritual development. It is rare indeed that someone approaches the end of the "worldling" designation and has the opportunity to become a "noble one."

THE INSIGHT LEADING TO EMERGENCE

Our mind has now reached the point at which it is recoiling from its entanglements with the mundane world and is deeply yearning for the experience of spiritual freedom. Although we have recognized the inherent danger of being swept away by our sensory experience, at this stage it is still possible to break the precepts, lose concentration, and become confused. The empty nature of phenomena has been seen, but we are still apt to be led astray by the insidious view of "self" that lurks in the deep recesses of our mind. It now becomes obvious that the final release from this predicament can only be achieved through the direct realization of the supramundane.

It is at this point that the insight leading to emergence arises. With the knowledge of equanimity toward formations and the knowledge of conformity as its foundation, the mind "emerges" from its grasping of conditioned formations and takes the unconditioned, nibbana, as its object.

Up until this point, we have been observing the impermanent, unsatisfactory, or selfless nature of each object as it arose to consciousness. When the insight leading to emergence appears, one of these three characteristics will become predominant in our mind, and will act as the doorway through which the unconditioned will be experienced.

Nibbana can realized in three ways. By discerning the impermanence of formations, one can realize nibbana as the elimination of the illusion of permanence. By discerning the unsatisfactory nature of formations, one can experience nibbana as the ending of all desires. By discerning the selfless nature of formations, one can realize nibbana as void or empty of self. The specific characteristic that will arise for each of us is dependent upon the natural proclivity of our mind.

THE CHANGE OF LINEAGE

In Gestalt psychology there is a visual phenomenon referred to as "figure/ground perception." The basic principle is that when we are focused on an object in the foreground of our perceptual field (the "figure"), we cannot at the same time see what is in the background (the "ground"). If at some point our focus changes and we become aware of that which had previously been in the background, we can no longer experience the figure, apparent to us just a moment ago.

The same principle applies to our spiritual awareness. As long as the mind is focusing its attention on conditioned phenomena, it cannot experience the unconditioned reality, which is always present as the background of our experience. However, as the stages of purification reveal the unsatisfactory nature of all conditioned formations, and the mind eventually ceases to focus upon them, the direct experience of the unconditioned reality naturally arises.

The mind's turning away from formations and taking nibbana as its object is referred to as the change of lineage. We are in the process of being transformed from the worldling status to the "lineage" of the noble ones. Nibbana is the object, but the mind is still, at this point, mundane. The defilements or fetters binding the mind to the sense world are not yet eradicated, but the realization of the supramundane path, which will destroy the defilements, is certain to occur.

THE PATH KNOWLEDGES

Path knowledge occurs when consciousness is associated with any of the four supramundane attainments, designated as the path of stream entry, the path of once-returning, the path of nonreturning, and the path of arahantship. When a path knowledge arises, both consciousness and the object of consciousness are supramundane, and the mind has reached a jhanic level of concentration. The path knowledges arise in sequence and each path knowledge arises only once. The knowledge lasts for one moment of consciousness and is immediately followed by a corresponding fruition knowledge.

There are no grades or levels to reality. As the Buddha has said, "Nibbana has only one taste: the taste of freedom." The four path knowledges merely indicate which defilements have been eradicated or reduced by virtue of that attainment and, according to the *Visuddhimagga*, the maximum number of lifetimes it will take until final liberation is achieved. At the moment of path knowledge, the four functions related to the Four Noble Truths are fulfilled: Suffering has been understood, craving has been abandoned, nibbana has been realized, and the Noble Eightfold Path has been fully developed.

The Path of Stream Entry

The first supramundane path knowledge is referred to as stream entry, since one has "entered the stream of consciousness" that leads to final liberation. No matter how prepared the mind is for the moment of stream entry, the experience is always sudden, spiritually illuminating, and transformational. During the experience, the mind has no perspective from which to observe what is occurring, since nibbana is void of any self to do the observation and void of any perspective from which to observe. The experience cannot be described because it is beyond the realm of ideas.

The path of stream entry eradicates three mental defilements or fetters: the personality view (the erroneous view of having a self), doubt about the efficacy of the Buddha's teaching, and the belief that by performing certain rites and rituals our mind will become purified.

According to the Buddha, a stream-enterer will have at most seven more lifetimes in the human or celestial realms before reaching the final path knowledge (that of arahantship). If this is true, it follows that there must be individuals who are already stream-enterers when they are born. This is actually the case. These individuals re-awaken in the midst of their lives when the causes and conditions are supportive of such an awakening. If they are not already on a spiritual path, they will immediately begin to seek one out. From an outside perspective, they appear to make rapid progress with their spiritual practices. What is actually occurring is the clearing away of the distorted perceptual overlays that have accumulated during this life, and the re-experiencing of insights that have been realized sometime in the past. At some point, stream-enterers will reach their "base level" of attainment and continue with their spiritual work. It is also possible, however, that some of these individuals will be prevented from recognizing their spiritual attainment because of circumstances resulting from unskillful kamma created in the past.

If there is no self in the experience of the unconditioned, we may wonder how peace, bliss, or freedom can actually be perceived. The unconditioned is *itself* peace, bliss, and freedom. Nibbana is actually freedom from the illusion that we are not already free. One meditator communicated about her experience as realizing, "Home is here, now...no words can describe it...just utterly 'wow' in the mantle of equanimity. Everything is secure. There is no danger...we haven't a care in the world. Nothing is risky; nothing can really be destroyed." Another meditator discovered that "There is no birth or death; who I am has never been born and will never die." These types of articulations arise after individuals return to the mundane level of consciousness; they are reflections of the experience of the supramundane state.

The Path of Once-Returning

The path of once-returning does not destroy any defilements but significantly reduces the unskillful roots of greed, hatred, and delusion. We will no longer react, as we did in the past, to the grosser levels of sensory experience.

The moment in which the path of once-returning is experienced is not as dramatic as the moment in which the path of stream entry is experienced. Consider a three-way bulb: With the first level of illumination, the darkness disappears. The subsequent levels of light simply make the room brighter. Similarly, after the initial illumination that arises through the experience of the unconditioned, our spiritual clarity just keeps getting brighter.

After reaching the path of stream entry, the experience of the unconditioned may still be viewed as being "out there," something that "we" want to experience again. However, when the path moment of once-returning is experienced, another shift in our understanding takes place. We now realize that we already are that for which we have been searching. In other words, a tacit understanding arises that the unconditioned is the only thing there is. Our viewpoint changes from trying to "realize" nibbana to one of learning how to stabilize our transcendent perspective. According to the Buddha, a once-returner will be born only once more in the sensual plane of existence before becoming an arahant.

The Path of Nonreturning

Even after the moments in which the paths of stream entry and once-returning have been experienced and the selfless nature of the personality has been realized, the conditioned mind still refuses to surrender its control. The mind resists dying to the recognition that it does not really "know" anything. Of course the mind has knowledge, but that knowledge is always based on what was true in the past. Every moment has its own wisdom to it. The conditioned mind prevents us from living out of the spontaneity that arises when we are truly present with each moment of experience.

The moment in which we experience the path of nonreturning fully eradicates the fetters of sense desire and ill will, the basic ways in which the mind has previously asserted itself when encountering sensory experience. The incompatibility of trying to maintain control and truly living in the present has now become crystal clear. Although there are still fetters that remain, consciousness is no longer being pushed and pulled about by forms of greed or hatred, and it is choiceless awareness that primarily defines our experience. The nonreturner will no longer take birth in the sensual plane, but will continue the work of becoming an arahant in a higher realm of existence.

The Path of Arahantship

The moment in which the path of arahantship is experienced eliminates the last of the fetters: desire for birth in the fine material realm, desire for birth in the immaterial realm, conceit, mental restlessness, and spiritual ignorance. Conceit is defined as pride or the comparing attitude of the mind. With personality view having been eradicated at the path of stream entry, we may wonder how conceit can still be present in the mind. Although the conditioned nature of the five aggregates has been thoroughly recognized, there remains, up until the moment of arahantship, a subtle belief that although there is no self, we still "exist" in some manner. But at this point in our spiritual development, all ideas of having a separate existence cease, along with all residual elements of conceit.

The arahant, having destroyed the roots and branches of spiritual ignorance will not be born again. As long as the arahant is alive, however, the mind and body will continue functioning. Past kamma will continue to come to fruition, but the arahant will no longer suffer, since craving, the cause of suffering, has been thoroughly abandoned. The arahant will no longer create new kamma, since spiritual ignorance, the primary condition for kamma, has been destroyed. According to the *Visuddhimagga*, when the arahant dies, the mind and body process ceases to function, and there is no rebirth in the future. To ask where the arahant goes after he or she dies is not a pertinent question, since there is no self that has ever gone anywhere. Just as a fire is extinguished after its fuel is gone, an arahant no longer comes to birth since the causes and conditions that perpetuated the cycle of birth and death are no longer operative.

THE FRUITION KNOWLEDGES

Fruition knowledge immediately follows the realization of each path moment and takes nibbana as its object. There is a fruition knowledge that corresponds to each of the path attainments. The initial fruition knowledge can be described as the experience of freedom and bliss that arises after the enormous effort expended to reach any of the path moments subsides.

Although each path knowledge is experienced only once, the fruition knowledges can be experienced many times. We can train the mind to deliberately enter into the fruition knowledge and remain in that supramundane state for minutes or even hours.

We are only able to experience the fruition attainment that corresponds to the stage of path knowledge we have realized. It is similar to the experience of climbing a mountain, stopping at each of its three base camps before finally ascending to the summit. Without reaching the higher elevations, we are limited to the views we can see from the particular base camp we have reached.

THE KNOWLEDGE OF REVIEWING

After the attainment of each path knowledge and the fruition knowledge that immediately follows, the mind automatically looks back and describes to itself what just transpired. Sometimes this review takes place immediately after the experience, as the mind seeks to gain a foothold on what just occurred. At other times, the review is completed after the immediate bliss of the experience has subsided. The process of trying to discern what transpired when the cognitive function of the mind was absent—when nibbana was realized—is referred to as the knowledge of reviewing.

The mind reviews the path, the fruition, and nibbana itself. The path is reviewed by recognizing the process that led up to the cessation of the conditioned formations and to the experience of the unconditioned. The fruition is reviewed by recognizing that consciousness was in a blissful and peaceful state of freedom before it emerged and started the review process. Nibbana is reviewed by recognizing that it has become a direct experience, opposed to a mental construct, and that it is void or empty of all conditioned formations. For some meditators, there is also a review of the defilements that have already been abandoned, and those that still need to be eradicated.

REACHING THE HIGHER PATHS AND FRUITION ATTAINMENTS

After developing the skill that enables us to abide in the first fruition attainment for extended periods of time, we should direct our efforts to achieving the further levels of spiritual development. It will not be as difficult to reach the higher stages as it was to reach the original path and fruition knowledges, but the work ahead is still quite challenging.

We must continue to practice in an environment that will support the development of our virtue, concentration, and wisdom. The balance between the spiritual faculties needs to be even more finely tuned since penetrating the more subtle and deeply rooted defilements requires a mental effort as focused as a laser's beam. Concentration and effort must be in perfect harmony, while faith and discrimination must work to keep the mind motivated and attentive. As always, mindfulness needs to orchestrate the functioning of each pair of factors. By practicing in this manner, the next higher path and fruition knowledge will have the opportunity to arise.

Our ultimate goal is to reach the path and fruition attainment of arahantship. When this occurs, we will "roar the lion's roar" of all the arahants: "Birth is destroyed, the holy life has been lived, what had to be done has been done, there is no more coming to any state of being." When, as an arahant, we can make this statement, all seven stages of purification have been fulfilled, and we have finally reached the pinnacle of spiritual development.

THE PATH GOES NOWHERE

For the last eight chapters, I have been describing the Buddha's *Path of Purification.* The concept of a path implies, of course, that a kind of actual journey is taking place. It implies that there is a beginning point, a given distance to traverse, and a destination that we will arrive at, given sufficient time and effort. However, this is not precisely the case.

The spiritual truth that we have been describing is already present and can be realized in this exact place. We have used the concepts of practice and effort to refer to a process that naturally unfolds. There is no need to *practice* becoming what we already are. In fact, in some ways, making an effort can actually be an impediment to realization. What is required is to merely cease identifying with the striving mind and to become aware of the self-existent truth of things as they are right here and right now. The act of striving creates a false dichotomy between the one who is striving and that which is being sought. We already are that for which we have been seeking.

The *Path of Purification* is a description of what occurs as part of the spiritual unfolding process, rather than a prescription of what needs to be accomplished by us. At the heart of the Buddha's teaching is the experience of selflessness. *Who* is there to practice and to follow any path? There are merely causes and conditions that create the results that we see in our lives.

The Buddha's purpose of outlining this natural unfolding process in terms of a path with all its associated practices is to describe the set of conditions which support the further opening of the mind and heart. This dynamic path is clearly mapped out for us in exquisite detail in the *Visuddhimagga*.

The greatest freedom is freedom from the illusion that we are not already free. When the veils of spiritual delusion begin to lift, we realize several things: ultimate truth is outside of time, the labels we attribute to phenomena are not the things themselves, all self-images are obstructions to seeing spiritual truth, life is similar to a waking dream, and the only true meditation practice is "non-meditation." We will explore each of these ideas in turn.

LIVING OUTSIDE OF TIME

Spiritual truth is realized in the present moment, which is, in fact, outside of time. Time is merely a concept and as such, it has no objective existence. Yet, when we objectify the concept of time, we convince ourselves of its existence based upon the apparent passage of time displayed by clocks.

There is no way to separate time from our thoughts about it. Our past, for example, is merely the reflection of our memories. Without our memories, we would have no "past." Many of us are psychologically burdened by painful histories, which are actually nothing more than thoughts in the mind with which we mistakenly identify. Nothing has ever happened to "you." What can happen to a concept or an image? A *victim mentality* occurs when we give more credence to our thoughts of the past than to our present-moment experience.

For many people, the story of their lives is not fully satisfying. They did not foresee life turning out the way that it did: the divorce, the death of a loved one, an unfulfilling career, and so forth. It is because we want the opportunity to have our life story end like a Hollywood movie, "happily ever after," that the idea of having a *future* becomes important to us. At the same time, we are frightened of the future because it will surely bring about our death. As a result of these two opposing forces, we tend to live in a psychological dilemma, whereby we are drawn to the future and, at the same time, fear its approach. Many of us live with this conflict all of the time. However, if there were no desire and no fear, there would not be any future. Once again, the future is nothing more than thoughts in the mind.

The greatest enemy to the conditioned mind is the reality of the present moment. The mind is always trying to oppose this experience, since the mind only lives through thoughts of the past and the future. The height of irrationality is saying "no" to what is taking place in the present moment—denying the only true reality.

Time and self are related ideas. We believe in time because we believe that there is a self that endures. When we let go of our identification with our self-constructs, we live in the true present moment, outside of time.

LABELS ARE NOT REALITIES

As we begin to recognize our inherent spiritual freedom, one form of confusion that clears is the tendency to react emotionally to the labels we use to describe our sense experiences. We react to our labels as if they were actually part of those experiences we encounter. Consider, for example, the sense experience we label as *automobile*.

If we analyze an automobile, on even a superficial level, we see that it is merely a combination of parts such as an engine, transmission, steering wheel, tires, fenders, and so forth. If we remove each of the parts in succession, we will find the "automobile" does not exist beyond the combination of its components. There will be nothing left but space. If we look even deeper into each of the parts, we will see that they are composed of atoms, molecules, and, on the deepest level, nothing but energy. When we confuse the imputation (or label) with the sense experience of seeing a particular form, we may say that it (in this case the automobile) is beautiful. As a consequence, we become attached to it, long to own it, and suffer if the automobile is lost, damaged, or stolen.

Our ability to differentiate between sense experiences and the labels we ascribe to them becomes even more essential when we talk about the body and mind that we identify as being our "self." When we deeply analyze this psychophysical organism, we find only a physical form, feelings, perceptions, mental formations, and consciousness. Each of these attributes can be further investigated until we discover that there is nothing within or behind them but emptiness. However, by believing that the labels are part of the actual experience, we may think that we (or others) are beautiful, creative, intelligent, and so forth. As a result of this misapprehension, we become attached to the body and mind and suffer when we age, become ill, or are in the process of dying.

THE INHERENT LIMITATIONS OF ANY SELF-IMAGE

Our self-image is the totality of who we believe we are and of what we believe we are capable of achieving. Our actions in life are a reflection of this image. We will strive to achieve what we believe we are capable of achieving, and will sabotage our results when our achievements are not consonant with what we believe we deserve. Most of the psychological work in the world is focused on improving, reprogramming, or reconditioning our self-image.

As we grow up, an initial self-image is formed in our mind. This first image became a point of reference for the future. If this initial image had some elements of inadequacy, we may have been trying to establish another self-image to prove that we are not inadequate. By attempting to negate the first image we are actually resisting it, which sets up an internal war that we cannot win. We would not be trying to create a new self-image unless we actually believed in the prior one.

As we continue to see more clearly from a spiritual perspective, we recognize the limitations of maintaining any self-image. As long as we are concerned with improving our sense of self, we will always have a "self" to improve. No matter what self-image we create for ourselves, it ultimately limits our ability to recognize our inherent freedom, which lies beyond all self-constructed images and boundaries. Any and all self-images affect our experience of freedom. We ultimately want to rest in the spaciousness that is present prior to identifying with any form of beliefs or images.

LIFE AS A WAKING DREAM

Several years ago there was a news program that featured a man who kept journals of everything he did. Every activity he engaged in during the day was recorded, including such entries as turning on a lamp, making his lunch, answering the phone, and using the bathroom. He had been keeping this record for many years and his journals filled his apartment. He believed that this "story" of his life was significant.

In actuality, we believe a version of same thing. We may not record everything we do, but we are constantly telling ourselves stories about our lives. These stories can take many forms. Some stories are about the physical body. We may believe that it is "my" hair, eyes, smile, or shape; that it is "I" who sits, walks, lies down, breathes, or hears sounds; and that it is "I" who gets old, becomes ill, and dies. Other stories are about the mind. We may believe that it is "I" who recognizes objects and people; that it is "I' who likes and dislikes experiences; that it is "I" who feels restless, guilty, or worried; and that it is "I" who thinks, experiences emotions, plans for the future, and perhaps it is "I" who becomes enlightened.

However, all these ideas of self have no footing in reality. One modern Zen master summed it up like this: "Why are we unhappy? Because 99% of everything we think, say, and do is for our self—and there isn't one!" While it is true that there is seeing, hearing, feeling, speaking, thinking, and so forth, there is no self as part of, behind, or in control of those processes.

Any tension, anxiety, or concern that we experience in our lives comes from believing that there is a self and if that self just worked hard enough and were smart enough everything would turn out perfectly. The mind tells us, "If I let go of my attempt to control my life, everything I am working towards will fall apart." In actuality, life will continue to unfold in the ways in which it has been unfolding.

As we grow spiritually it becomes clear to us that *we* are not living our lives. Our lives are being lived through these bodies and minds. We superimpose our story over what is occurring, as if we were independent selves and in control of our lives. It is all just a story, merely a play of consciousness.

After a sleeping dream, when the dreamer awakes, the dreaming ends. There is no question that the dream self and the dream characters are mere constructions of the mind. As we awake from this living dream, there is a corresponding realization that our self and the other characters in life with whom we interact are also dream images and constructions of the conditioned mind.

In order to live our lives on a daily basis, we need to act as if we were in control, while at the same time knowing that we are not. If we decided to do nothing and let life unfold by itself, we would still be deciding to do something, which in this case would be nothing. We all have a sense of precognition as to how our lives are unfolding. We make our plans based upon that intuitive sense of direction. What changes in our experience is that there is no longer an attachment to any outcome.

THE PRACTICE OF NON-MEDITATION

As was stated at the beginning of this chapter, spiritual truth is always already present. Throughout this book we have used concepts of practice and effort to describe a natural unfolding process. At the ultimate level of practice, which is not really practice at all, the rational, linear, and cognitive mind is left behind, as are all models of spiritual development. We drop our identification with both the objects of consciousness and with the frames of consciousness that are observing the objects that are arising and falling away.

We are left with a silent spaciousness that is beyond the concepts of silence and spaciousness. There is awareness present but there is no "one" who is being aware. This awareness is so empty of concepts that it is no longer considered to be awareness. We no longer cling to anything—not even to non-clinging.

Non-meditation is beyond all forms of thought construction, and even beyond the idea of stillness. There is no "doing it right." There is no center or edge to this practice or experience. The moment we believe that we are practicing non-meditation, we are no longer practicing it. Non-meditation and ultimate freedom are one and the same.

All paths, religions, and spiritual practices are just more stories. There is ultimately nothing that we need to do or practice since we are already free. And, again, the greatest freedom is freedom from the illusion that we are not already free—and all maps of the true spiritual journey lead us right to where we are.

AFTERWORD: LIVING AN ENLIGHTENED LIFE

Everything that arises, disappears; whatever is born, dies. Nothing escapes the cycle of birth and death. It is important for us to directly and experientially realize that there is never a point in time when something "exists" and is not in the process of becoming something other than it was just a moment before. All suffering comes from attachment—trying to hold on to that which is perpetually changing—and all attachment comes from delusion. We need to learn to live in the clarity and space of non-attachment, neither grasping nor pushing anything away. The key is to just be present with what arises from moment to moment without holding or resisting. At the same time, it is essential not to fall into the trap of denying the relative existence of the five aggregates and the world of experience they present.

Compassion is the willingness to play in the field of dreams even though you are awake. Approach life with joy, enthusiasm, love, and an open heart. Take delight in the manifestations of life: It is all a play of consciousness and it is really all play. If something appears serious or burdensome—even death—then we are lost in delusion. The "field of dreams" is this world of the senses with all its myriad forms. Being awake is the direct know-ing that there is no one who suffers, no one who is born and no one who dies. It is the five aggregates that are born and die. Who we are has never been born and never dies.

In actuality, there is no one who is expressing compassion to anyone else. It is all part of the play. The world is our mir-ror. There is only consciousness rising and falling along with its objects; it is all selfless. Whatever we see as being real is a pro-jection of our own mind. It is where our mind is stuck or iden-tified with the illusion.

Nothing exists—not even nothing. Existence and non-existence are both concepts. Not holding anywhere is free-dom beyond measure.

We must die to each moment and allow life to express itself through us. Our lives may not turn out the way in which the ego has imagined, but when we surrender to the truth of what is, we will find freedom beyond measure as surely as the river finds its way to the sea. When we move beyond the dualistic world, there is a rebirth into the deathless. We finally come home to a place that we have really never left.

BIBLIOGRAPHY

Bodhi, Bhikkhu (ed.). *A Comprehensive Manual of Abhidhamma*. Kandy, Sri Lanka: Buddhist Publication Society, 1993.

————. *The Mahasatipatthana Sutta*. Audio tapes of talks by Bhikkhu Bodhi. Boston: Dharma Seed Tape Library, (approx.) 1995.

————. *The Noble Eightfold Path*. Kandy, Sri Lanka: Buddhist Publication Society, 1994.

————. *Transcendental Dependent Arising*. Kandy, Sri Lanka: Buddhist Publication Society, 1980.

Buddhaghosa, Bhadantacariya. *The Path of Purification*. 2 vols. Translated by Bhikkhu Nyanamoli. Boulder: Shambhala Publications, 1976.

Flickstein, Matthew. *Journey to the Center*. Boston: Wisdom Publications, 1998.

Gunaratana, Mahathera Henepola. *The Jhanas in Theravada Buddhist Meditation*. Kandy, Sri Lanka: Buddhist Publication Society, 1998.

Gunaratna, V. F. *Rebirth Explained*. Kandy, Sri Lanka: Buddhist Publication Society, 1980.

Khema, Ayya. *Who Is My Self?* Boston: Wisdom Publications, 1997.

Ledi, Sayadaw. *Manual of Mindfulness of Breathing*. Kandy, Sri Lanka: Buddhist Publication Society, 1999.

Mahaniranonda, Aachan Naeb. *Vipassana Bhavana*. Bangkok, Thailand: The Post Publishing Company, 1985.

Mahasi, Sayadaw. *The Progress of Insight*. Kandy, Sri Lanka: Buddhist Publication Society, 1978.

Namto, Achan Sobin. *Manual for Checking Insight Meditation Progress*. North Hollywood: Wat Thai of Los Angeles, 1985.

Nanamoli, Bhikkhu and Bhikkhu Bodhi, trans. *The Middle Length Discourses of the Buddha*. Boston: Wisdom Publications, 1995.

Nanarama, Mahathera. *The Seven Stages of Purification and the Insight Knowledges*. Kandy, Sri Lanka: Buddhist Publication Society, 1983.

Pandita, Sayadaw U. *In This Very Life*. Boston: Wisdom Publications, 1993.

Piyadassi, Thera. *The Seven Factors of Enlightenment*. Kandy, Sri Lanka: Buddhist Publishing Society, 1960.

Silananda, Ven. U. *The Four Foundations of Mindfulness*. Boston: Wisdom Publications, 1990.

Soma, Bhikkhu. *The Way of Mindfulness*. Kandy, Sri Lanka: Buddhist Publication Society, 1981.

Walshe, Maurice, trans. *The Long Discourses of the Buddha*. Boston: Wisdom Publications, 1987.

INDEX

ABOUT THE AUTHOR

Matthew Flickstein has been a practicing psychotherapist and insight meditation teacher for over twenty-four years. A psychotherapist for most of his professional career, Matthew has created many personal development workshops and has trained thousands of people. He has also certified other psychotherapists to lead stress management and personal development workshops that he created. For many years he was a therapist in private practice specializing in intensive short-term interventions.

Matthew earned his B.S. degree from the University of Maryland, an M.S. degree in Counseling and Psychotherapy from Loyola College, and completed Ph.D. coursework at the Saybrook Institute. He interned at Johns Hopkins Counseling and Psychiatric Center in Baltimore.

In 1984, Matthew co-founded the Bhavana Society, a Buddhist monastic center in West Virginia, with Bhante Gunaratana. He was subsequently ordained and lived at the center as a Theravadan Buddhist monk. Matthew is the founder and resident teacher of the Forest Way Insight Meditation Center in the Blue Ridge Mountains of Virginia, which specializes in long-term retreats for lay practitioners.

Matthew is the author of *Journey to the Center: A Meditation Workbook* and a co-editor of the best-selling meditation manual *Mindfulness in Plain English* by Bhante Gunaratana. He currently lives in Ruckersville, Virginia.

ABOUT WISDOM PUBLICATIONS

Wisdom Publications, a nonprofit publisher, is dedicated to making available authentic works relating to Buddhism for the benefit of all. We publish books by ancient and modern masters in all traditions of Buddhism, translations of important texts, and original scholarship. Additionally, we offer books that explore East-West themes unfolding as traditional Buddhism encounters our modern culture in all its aspects. Our titles are published with the appreciation of Buddhism as a living philosophy, and with the special commitment to preserve and transmit important works from Buddhism's many traditions.

To learn more about Wisdom, or to browse books online, visit our website at www.wisdompubs.org.

You may request a copy of our catalog online or by writing to this address:

Wisdom Publications
199 Elm Street
Somerville, Massachusetts 02144 USA
Telephone: 617-776-7416
Fax: 617-776-7841
Email: info@wisdompubs.org
www.wisdompubs.org

The Wisdom Trust

As a nonprofit publisher, Wisdom is dedicated to the publication of Dharma books for the benefit of all sentient beings and dependent upon the kindness and generosity of sponsors in order to do so. If you would like to make a donation to Wisdom, you may do so through our website or our Somerville office. If you would like to help sponsor the publication of a book, please write or email us at the address above.

Thank you.

Wisdom is a nonprofit, charitable 501(c)(3) organization affiliated with the Foundation for the Preservation of the Mahayana Tradition (FPMT).